# THE DIVINE SERVICE

OF THE HOLY EIGHTH ŒCUMENICAL COUNCIL

Icon of the Eighth Œcumenical Council, St. Stephen's Monastery, Meteora

# THE DIVINE SERVICE

of the Holy Eighth Œcumenical Council

Convoked in Constantinople
in the Years of Our Lord 879–880

Composed by the Nun Thecla of Saint Stephen's Monastery,
Also containing the Presentation of Metropolitan
Hierotheos of Naupactus
on its Recognition,
and the Encyclical of Metropolitan
Seraphim of Piraeus
on its Celebration.

Translated by Gregory Heers

Uncut Mountain Press

## THE DIVINE SERVICE
of the Holy Eighth Œcumenical Council
© 2024.
Uncut Mountain Press

All rights reserved under International and Pan-American Copyright Conventions.

uncutmountainpress.com

The Divine Service of the Holy Eighth Œcumenical Council.—1ˢᵗ ed.
Written by Nun Thecla of St. Stephen's Monastery, Meteora.
Translated by Gregory Heers.

ISBN: 978-1-63941-033-0

I. Eastern Orthodox Church
II. Eastern Orthodox Christian Worship
III. Service Text

*The Eighth Council's Fathers truly wise,
speaking with great clarity,
have proven heralds of godly truth,
condemning heresies
and the Latin dogmas.*

Detail from the Icon of the Eighth Œcumenical Council
at St. Stephen's Monastery, Meteora Greece.

# CONTENTS

On the recognition of the council convoked in Constantinople in the year of our Lord 879-880 as the Eighth Œcumenical by Metropolitan of Naupactus and St. Blaise, HIEROTHEOS ............................ 9

Criteria of the Œcumenicity of a Council ............................ 33

Historic Confirmations to the Council of 879-880 being Œcumenical .................................................................. 37

Pastoral Encyclical of the Metropolitan of Piraeus, SERAPHIM, on the Institution of the Celebration of the Memory of the Holy Fathers of the Eighth Œcumenical Council ............................................................. 43

THE DIVINE SERVICE of the Holy Eighth Œcumenical Council ............................................................. 53

Metropolitan Hierotheos of Naupactus & St. Blaise

# PRESENTATION

## On the recognition of the council convoked in Constantinople in the year of our Lord 879-880 as the Eighth Œcumenical

By His Eminence Metropolitan Hierotheos of Naupactus & St. Blaise

before the Synod of the Church of Greece
on the 6th of October 2011

Most Blessed President,
Most Reverend Hierarchs,

Warmly do I thank the Holy and Sacred Synod for assigning to me the examination of this matter, which is a serious one. I feel that I shall not be fully able to meet its expectations; I shall simply provide the stimulus for further discussion. It is, nevertheless, my hope that the good judgment and knowledge of my revered and beloved brethren, and especially of the academic bishops, will fill the gaps which this presentation may contain. I also thank the Sacred Synod for giving me the chance to study a topic which I had wanted to explore more for a long time now and with which I am conversant.

I consider it important that for the first time such a topic is laid before the gatherings of the Hierarchy of the Church of Greece, and this has been hailed with particular theological satisfaction. This, your beatitude, is accounted among the positive works of your archbishopric. It is within the jurisdiction of the supreme Body of the Church to discuss such serious issues, and in this way the conscience of the Church is expressed.

## 1. The term "Œcumenical"

Before we proceed to the examination of the entire matter, we must give some explanations which will help in more fully understanding it. *Imprimis* we must look at the meaning of the term 'œcumenical'.

Fr. George Florovsky has noted that the original meaning of the term 'œcumenical' was probably 'imperial'.[1] The Roman Empire stretched over the whole known world of that time, over the whole known 'inhabited earth' (*œcumene*); hence whatever pertained to the Empire was called œcumenical. Thus, the term 'œcumenical' was given to those that had some general mission in the Empire and reported to the Empire; e.g. the Prosecutor, the Inspector, etc. were called œcumenical.[2]

Within this context, the Bishop of New Rome, the city where the seat of the Roman Senate and of the Emperor was, obtained the title 'œcumenical', and by extension the general council, which went beyond the local ones, was called œcumenical. This will be better illustrated by what is to follow in the next section.

## 2. Local and Œcumenical Councils

From the very beginning of the Church, the Apostles were faced with various issues which they had to solve, for which purpose they came together in gatherings or councils such as the first Apostolic Council of Jerusalem in A.D. 48.

Referring to the Œcumenical Councils, Professor John Karmiris writes that they are the "highest authority" in the Church and that they "were convoked by the emperors", mainly because of dogmatic

---

[1] Georges Florovsky, *Bible, Church, Tradition: An Eastern Orthodox View*, Collected Works: Vol. 1 (Büchervertriebsanstalt: Vaduz 1987), p. 95.

[2] Fr. John Romanides, see in Metropolitan Hierotheos of Naupactus (Nafpaktos), *Empirical Dogmatics*, vol. 2, 2nd ed., (Nativity of the Theotokos Monastery [Pelagia]: 2011), p. 446.

controversies, and that representatives of all the local churches participated therein.³

This precisely shows that the Œcumenical Councils have three things in common. First, they concern themselves with determining dogmatic matters, such as the Trinitarian dogma, the Christological dogma, and the concomitant dogmas on the honour of the sacred images.⁴ Second, they were convoked by the emperors. Thus, the First Œcumenical was convoked by Constantine the Great, the Second by Theodosius the Great, the Third by Theodosius the Younger, the Fourth by Marcian and Pulcheria, the Fifth by Justinian I, the Sixth by Constantine Pogonatus, the Quinisext by Justinian II, and the Seventh by Constantine VI with Irene of Athens. Let it be emphasized that the Emperors avoided exercising any right of intervention in the dogmatic or other discussions of the Fathers of the Œcumenical Councils, who passed judgement in the Holy Spirit.⁵ The third is that all the local church participate.

Of great importance is the conversation of Saint Maximus the Confessor with Theodosius, the bishop of Caesarea-in-Bithynia, regarding theological matters, with reference also to the Councils. At one point, when Saint Maximus referred to an Orthodox council that took place in Rome, Bishop Theodosius replied that this council was not valid because "it had not been summoned by the emperor's decree." Then Saint Maximus analyzed the question of the relationship between right faith and imperial decrees. Having referred to councils that were convoked by imperial decrees and yet were condemned "for the godlessness of the dogmas which they impiously confirmed," he asks: "Which canon bids that only those councils be approved which were assembled by the command of an emperor, or that councils are to be assembled by imperial command at all?" There is no canon decreeing that we accept as councils only those that are assembled by imperial orders. On the contrary, the [37th Apostolic] canon decreed that a council (that is, a local council)

---

3  John Karmiris, *The Dogmatic and Symbolic Monuments of the Orthodox Catholic Church*, vol. I, (Athens 1960), p. 106.

4  Ibid, p. 107.

5  Ibid. p. 108.

be held "twice per year in every province," "without making any mention of imperial decrees," and this local council works for the security "of our salvific faith and for the correction of all things not agreeing with the divine law of the Church." Saint Maximus then concludes, "The pious canon of the Church recognises as holy and accepted those councils which were distinguished for rightness of dogmas."[6]

From this passage from Saint Maximus it becomes abundantly clear that the canons of the Church call for the convocation of local councils which are concerned with dogmatic matters, not for councils that are convoked by imperial decrees. Moreover, it is clear that it is the Orthodox dogmas and not simply the convocation by imperial decrees that proves a council to be Orthodox.

In his study on "the authority of the ancient councils and the tradition of the Fathers" and especially in the section on "the councils in the early Church," Fr. George Florovsky refers to the history of councils in general and more specifically of the Œcumenical Councils. He claims that in the ancient Church there was no "Conciliar theory" or any complex "theology of the Councils," nor were there any "fixed canonical regulations;" rather, the councils of the Church in the first centuries "were occasional meetings, convened for special purposes, usually in the situation of urgency, to discuss particular matters of common concern." Usually the bishops of a region would gather to elect and ordain new bishops, and this became the foundation of the "future Provincial and Metropolitan system." It seems that councils appeared in Asia Minor towards the end of the 2$^{nd}$ century, while in North Africa also "a kind of Conciliar system was established in the third century." Thus, in the ancient Church, councils "were *events*, rather than an institution."[7]

The bishops of each region would assemble in councils to elect bishops and to decide more general matters of the Church,

---

[6] Saint Maximus the Confessor, *Dogmatic and Anti-Heretical, Liturgical Writings - Life of Maximus, Philokalia of the Watchful and Ascetical Fathers* (Thessalonica: Patristic Publications "Gregory Palamas",1995), vol. 15c, pp. 26-28.

[7] Fr. George Florovsky, ibid. p. 94.

according to the 34th Apostolic Canon. As time went on, to better organise the Church they adopted the diocesan division of the Roman Empire into provinces and exarchies, so as to preserve the conciliar system of the Church which functioned in various ways ever since the day of Pentecost, as is proven by the first Apostolic Council of Jerusalem but also by the way in which the Divine Liturgy is celebrated. In this way they constituted the unity of the Church and developed the metropolitan system and later the patriarchal system of ecclesiastical governance. This was done by the Fathers of the Church with the inspiration of the All-Holy Spirit.

When the Roman Empire became Christian, then it became apparent that "Church was co-extensive with Commonwealth," whereupon the œcumenicity of the Commonwealth rendered manifest the œcumenicity of the Church. It was within this framework that the Great Council in Nicea was also convoked, which became the model for all the other councils. The local churches had to learn to live not "as self-contained units" but "as parts of a vast spiritual government."[8]

Fr. George Florovsky characteristically notes: "It will be no exaggeration to suggest that Councils were never regarded as a canonical institution, but rather as occasional *charismatic events*."[9] The Church herself is "an assembly, which is never adjourned," while the Council or the "Conciliar institution… is *de jure Divino*… in so far as it happens to be a true image or manifestation of the Church herself."[10] In the end, "the Council is not above the Church" but is the manifestation of the Church and her "representation." For this reason, oftentimes the decisions of councils "were accepted or rejected in the Church not on formal or 'canonical' ground. And the verdict of the Church has been highly selective."[11]

On this topic, Fr. John Romanides would teach that the Œcumenical Council never was a canonical institution in the Church, as were the local councils, whose times of assembly

---

8    Ibid. p. 95.

9    Ibid. p. 96.

10   Ibid. pp. 96-97.

11   Ibid. p. 97.

were defined by the holy canons, but were rather the result of the recognition of the Church as the official state religion. This means that the emperors wished to be informed of the view of the Church on a given dogmatic matter and then these decisions were made into laws of the state, according the Roman jurisprudence.[12] [13]

The heretics were condemned by the local councils and their decisions were shared with other local churches. This was done in the ancient Church. When, however, Christianity became the religion of the Roman State, then the Emperor wished to know the faith of the Church and to ratify it by law so that there might be unity in the Empire.[14]

For this reason, the canons of the Œcumenical Councils were not intended to replace the canons of the local councils. There were the canons of the local councils (either canons regarding the procedures of the [local] councils or the canons of the various [local] churches participating in the [general] council), and it was now a chance to standardise the common practice of the Church, to institute canons of Œcumenical Councils, which would be recognised by the State as the laws of the Churches. And this was done in the formulation of the faith.[15] The members of the Œcumenical Councils spoke and acted as representatives of their local churches and not as isolated individuals.[16]

In an age when there is no Emperor to convoke an Œcumenical Council, this can be done by the Œcumenical Patriarch, without it being considered an Œcumenical Council. That is why the council

---

12  Fr. John Romanides. "Church Councils and Civilization." Paper presented at the VI[th] Meeting of the Lutheran - Orthodox Joint Commission, May 31-June 8, 1991, Moscow. Published in Greek in *Theologia* vol. 66, no. 4 (1995): 646-680.

13  Fr. John Romanides, see in Metropolitan Hierotheos of Naupactus, *Empirical Dogmatics*, vol. 2, 2nd ed., published by Monastery of the Nativity of the Theotokos (Pelagia), 2011, pp. 436-437.

14  Ibid. p. 439.

15  Ibid. p. 441.

16  Ibid. pp. 443-444.

that is being prepared to be convoked is called "the Great and Holy Council."[17]

Referring to the topic of Œcumenical Councils, Bishop Athanasius Yevtich among other things also speaks of how they came into being and of their structure, but also of their importance for the life of the Church. Bearing in mind the views of various scientists, that because the Œcumenical Councils bear some external resemblance to "conferences of the Roman Senate," for this reason they served as a kind of "imperial *consilium*" regarding various matters of the Church, and could therefore be termed "imperial councils" of the "State Church" or the "Church of the Empire" of the Constantinean period, he claims that there were some external similarities with certain proceedings and judicial forms of the Roman Senate, but that nevertheless "the essential should not be confused with the non-essential in the conciliar system," because what characterizes the Œcumenical Councils is "the ecclesiastical basis", that is, "the conciliarity of the Church" which preëxisted in the life of the body of the Church. This can be seen in the tradition of the conciliar institution which was dominant in the ancient Church, in her later organisation, but also in the constitution of the local councils for confronting various problems in the Church during the first centuries. This preëxisting conciliarity of the Church also informed the manner in which Œcumenical Councils are convoked. Moreover, the Emperors would convoke the councils following the advice of the bishops; likewise, there are Œcumenical Councils that were attended neither by the emperors nor by their representatives.[18]

What Saint Nikodemos the Hagiorite writes on the difference between local and Œcumenical Councils and on how they are convoked is important. He notes that there are four characteristics of the Œcumenical Councils, three of which are common to local councils as well, but the one is "the essential, the constituent, and in fact the peculiar difference which distinguishes all Œcumenical

---

17  Ibid. p. 446.

18  Athanasius Yevtich, *Christ, the Beginning and the End*, (Goulandri-Horn Institute: Athens 1983), p. 149 et seq.

Councils." The first "distinguishing feature of all Œcumenical Councils" is "that they are convoked at the behest, not of the Pope or of such and such a patriarch, but by imperial orders." The second property is "that there be discussion concerning the Faith, and thereafter the exposition of a decision and a dogmatic decree [*horos*], which followed every single one of the Œcumenical Councils but also some local ones, as well." The third property is "that all dogmas and canons laid out thereby be Orthodox, pious, and concordant with the divine Scriptures or the previous Œcumenical Councils." On this point, the words of Saint Maximus the Confessor apply: "It is the pious faith that ratifies the councils that have been, and again, it is the rightness of dogmas that judges the councils." Finally, the fourth property is "that all Orthodox patriarchs and prelates of the Catholic Church agree and accept everything that has been decreed and ordained by the Œcumenical Councils, either by their personal presence or by their own legate or, in the absence of such a representative, by their letters." This consensus of the patriarchs is the constituent characteristic that renders these councils œcumenical, but also the distinguishing characteristics that differentiates the Œcumenical Council from the local one.[19]

There is also a difference between diocesan and local councils. A *diocesan* council is that which is constituted by the bishop or metropolitan or patriarch only with his clergymen, without other bishops, whereas a *local* council is when a metropolitan or patriarch meets together with his metropolitans or with his bishops and generally when the bishops of a province gather to examine common issues touching upon dogmatic and canonical matters.[20]

Consequently, the Œcumenical Councils constitute the highest authority in the Church, and although they are convoked by the emperor, nevertheless they are charismatic events, since in reality the gravity of the Œcumenical Councils is defined by the great dogmatic issues with which they deal and by the participation of

---

19  Saint Nikodemos the Hagiorite, *Rudder*, (Papademetriou: Athens 1970), pp. 118-119.

20  Ibid., pp. 366-367, note 2.

great Fathers or by the teaching of the Fathers on which they base themselves. Besides, the Fathers of the Church who reached theosis were enlightened by the Holy Spirit because they were in a spiritual state such as to be receptive of divine enlightenment.[21]

All this was said to make clear that the Œcumenical Council has as its foundation the local councils, since the local councils participate in the Œcumenical Council in their entirety. This means that even this present council (synod) of the bishops of the Church of Greece is a local council and not only could but should rule on dogmatic questions and on the particular matter at hand, i.e. that the council under Saint Photius the Great (879-880) and the one under Saint Gregory Palamas (1351) are respectively the Eighth and Ninth Œcumenical Councils, and then pass on this decision to the Pan-Orthodox Council, so that all the [local] churches may discuss and decide on this. Besides, both of the two basic issues with which the two councils, that of 879-880 and that of 1351, dealt, that is, the *Filioque* and the *actus purus*, are matters which the whole Orthodox Tradition, as expressed by the God-bearing Fathers of the Church, has considered to be heresies. Thus, it will be no novelty for us as a local church to accept these two councils as œcumenical and to propose their acceptance as such by the whole Orthodox Church; rather, it is within the realm of the workings of local councils.

After these introductory, informative remarks, I shall proceed to analyze the thesis that the council of the year 879-880 has all the characteristics of an Œcumenical Council and may be characterized as the Eighth Œcumenical Council.

## 3. The Council of the Year 879-880

The council that convened in Constantinople in the year 879-880, over which Saint Photius the Great presided and in which three hundred eighty-three Fathers participated from east and west representing the five ancient patriarchates, including the one of Old Rome, restored the peace and unity of the Church after various unpleasant events. This presentation does not purpose to refer to

---

21   Ibid., pp. 120-121.

those events, as I have already done so in other texts of mine.[22] The fact is that this council has all the elements that would justify its characterization as œcumenical. Wherefore thus has it been called by many Fathers and teachers, such as Theodore Balsamon, Nilus of Thessalonica, Nicholas Cabasilas, Nilus of Rhodes, Macarius of Ancyra, Saint Symeon of Thessalonica, Saint Mark Eugenicus of Ephesus, Joseph Bryennius, Gennadius Scholarius, Dositheus of Jerusalem, Constantine Oikonomos, *et alii*, but also by more recent ones, such as Chrysostom Papadopoulos, Archbishop of Athens, who wrote that this council has "not only the external but also all the internal features of an Œcumenical Council" and dealt with serious dogmatic issues, such as the addition of the *Filioque* and the primacy of the Bishop of Rome.[23]

This council is œcumenical and is so called because it was convoked by Emperor Basil the Macedonian, representatives of all the patriarchates attended it, Saint Photius the Great and the representatives of the Pope of Rome presided, it dealt with serious dogmatic and ecclesiological issues, and its decisions align with the teaching of the Prophets, Apostles, and Fathers of the Church; in other words, they are in harmony with the whole tradition of the Church.

The minutes of this council were published by Dositheus, Patriarch of Jerusalem, in his book *Tome of Joy*,[24] which was printed in Rimnik of Wallachia in September of the year 1705, a year and a half before Dositheus's death. For this edition of the minutes of the Eighth Œcumenical Council he used the 16th-century manuscript of the Monastery of Iveron.[25]

---

22  Metropolitan Hierotheos of Naupactus and St. Blaise, *Photius the Great and the Eighth Œcumenical Council*, 'Piraean Church' journal.

23  John Karmiris, *The Dogmatic…*, ibid., p. 262, and Bishop of Abydos Cyril Katerelos, *Rome and Papal Primacy during the Patriarchate of Ignatius and Saint Photius (847-886): the Eighth Œcumenical Council of the Roman Catholic Church (869-870)*, (Thessalonica 1998), p. 313 et seq.

24  Dositheus, *Tome of Joy* (Basil Regopoulos: Thessalonica 1995).

25  See Constantine Siamakis's introduction to Dositheus's *Tome of Joy*, ibid., p. 11.

A careful reading of the minutes of this council leads the reader to realize that the council proclaims itself œcumenical and is thus titled by the Emperors, Saint Photius the Great, the Pope's legates, and its members. The term "œcumenical" occurs dozens of time in the minutes. All the members of the council believe that they are the continuation of the Seventh Œcumenical Council, which they hence ratify as œcumenical. So the Seventh Œcumenical Council was ratified by this council that we are now examining and this, among other things, is a testament to its seriousness.

A significant dissertation on the topic of this important council has been written by the priest Philip Zymaris entitled "The Historical, Dogmatic, and Canonical Significance of the Council of Constantinople (879-880)", which has not been published.[26] I propose that the Apostolic Ministry of the Church of Greece publish it, for its importance. This dissertation was submitted in the Pastoral Department of the Theological School of the University of Thessalonica and was approved by it, while Professor and Metropolitan of Pergamus John Zizioulas was rapporteur. Upon carefully reading this dissertation, one realizes the great significance of the council which has been justly called Eighth Œcumenical.

The author commences with the realization that unfortunately in the West this important council has been considered either as a "false council" or as not having done work of any significance, that is, that "it did not proceed to make any dogmatic decision."[27] If one should read its minutes, however, he would be convinced "that in these Fathers there was a clear ecclesiological conscience."[28]

The goal of the dissertation in question is to ascertain "the ecclesiological importance of the council of 879-880, which was important for the Church and, ultimately, for the world today."[29] Finally, it is proven that "this council could be considered an exposition of ecclesiology," since all the topics that were discussed

---

26  Priest Philip Zymaris, *The Historical, Dogmatic, and Canonical Significance of the Council of Constantinople (879-880)*, Thessalonica, March 2000, unpublished.

27  Ibid., pp. 10-11.

28  Ibid., pp.10.

29  Ibid., pp. 15-14.

"have a common ecclesiological framework, and the decisions regarding these matters clearly indicate this specific ecclesiological consciousness, which is a continuation of the consciousness of the foregoing Fathers of the Church." The main topics of discussion at the council were five, namely, "first, the primacy of the Pope; second, the offices in the Church and their interrelationship; third, the local customs; fourth, the immediate raising of a layman to the rank of bishop [consecutive ordination]; and fifth, the *Filioque*."[30]

Also significant is the analysis of the councils of the year 869-870, which condemned Saint Photius, and of the year 879-880, which we are studying, done by the bishop of Abydos Cyril Katerelos in his study entitled "Rome and Papal Primacy during the Patriarchate of Ignatius and Saint Photius (847-886): the Eighth Œcumenical Council of the Roman Catholic Church (869-870)."[31]

At this point we shall need to briefly look at two of these topics so as to show the significance of this Œcumenical Council.

## *The Primacy of the Pope*

The first issue was the primacy of the Pope. The discussion that took place in the council between Saint Photius the Great, the Eastern bishops, but also the representatives of the pope clearly showed that the Pope does have primacy in the Church, but "with clear ecclesiological boundaries," as these are defined by the 34$^{th}$ Apostolic Canon; that is, he is first only with respect to seniority, "within and not above the Church. According to this view, each hierarch that does not keep the spirit of the Apostolic Canon places himself outside of the Church and is defrocked or excommunicated; the popes are no exception."[32]

The legates of the Pope at the council were maintaining that only Saint Peter and the Popes, his successors, have "the authority to bind and to loose, that is, priesthood. Therefore, the Pope, as the successor of the chief of the Apostles, is the only source of the

---

30   Ibid., p. 203.

31   Bishop of Abydos Cyril Katerelos, see above, footnote 23.

32   Ibid., pp. 78-80.

priesthood, and consequently, any authority that Photius happens to have does not proceed from his own archpriesthood [bishophood] but from the Pope."[33]

Saint Photius the Great and the Fathers of this council "supported primacy of honour (*presbeia timēs*) as a necessary ecclesiological principle for the preservation of the unity of the Church throughout the world; according to primacy of honour, however, the preservation of this unity is clearly not perceived as imposed by one *primus*, who is above the Church as an authority. This position is clearly expressed in an epistle of Photius, in which he emphasises the Orthodox interpretation of the Gospel passage Matthew 16:18-19. This interpretation leads to the crucial ecclesiological principle that each bishop is of equal honour with respect to his archpriesthood [bishophood]."[34] The Pope has the privilege of honour and must abide by the canons of the Church, while this privilege must be exercised within the spirit of the holy canons.[35] This means that the Pope has no jurisdiction in other ecclesiastical dioceses. When the Pope does not keep the canons and places himself above the Church, then he can be defrocked, as was done with Pope Nicholas I who was defrocked because he interfered with Constantinople and Bulgaria.[36]

So it appears that the primacy of the Pope, according to the Westerners, is founded not on a canonical and ecclesiological but on a dogmatic basis, namely, that the priesthood of the Pope is the fount of the priesthood of all the other patriarchs and bishops. That is precisely where the issue lies, not in the primacy of honour or the presidency of the council. This could never, nor can it now ever, be accepted by the Orthodox Church.

As one reads the minutes and the discussions that took place during the commencement of the council, he realizes that in the beginning there appear two kinds of ecclesiology, the Western, which viewed the Pope as the head of the whole Church, and the

---

33   Ibid., pp. 82-83.
34   Ibid., p. 81.
35   Ibid., p. 83.
36   Ibid., p. 204.

Eastern, which consists of the conciliar system of governance, on the basis of the holy canons and the tradition of the Church. The legates, it seems, tried to impose the Western kind of ecclesiology, but with the wisdom and the shrewd interventions of Patriarch Photius and of the other members, the Eastern ecclesiology fully prevailed, which is founded on the conciliar system of Church governance and on the non-interference of ecclesiastical dioceses in another ecclesiastical diocese.

Very telling in this regard is the first canon that this council drafted in its fifth act, which institutes the autonomy of each ecclesiastical diocese in matters of order and discipline. According to this canon, if any bishop, clergyman, or layman belonging to the Pope is punished by him, he is to be subjected to the same punishment also by the Patriarch of Constantinople, and vice versa. The canon concludes: "none of the privileges [*presbeia*] belonging to the most holy throne of the Church of the Romans or to her primate being at all changed or innovated, neither now nor hereafter."[37] This means the acceptance of the conciliar system of governance and that the primacy of the Pope is not a primacy of authority but a primacy of honour; in other words, the Pope is not the head of the whole Church, he is not the fount of priesthood, and therefore he has no jurisdiction in other ecclesiastical dioceses. According to Zonaras, "The fathers of the council did not wish the Pope of Elder Rome and the Patriarch of this new one, Constantinople, to be at variance with each other, but rather to be of one mind; for they were still of one faith and of one throne."[38]

This canon is of "crucial ecclesiological importance," since "it restores a 'eucharistic' view of the ecclesiastical structure throughout the world." The ecclesiastical importance of this canon lies not only in that it stresses the equality of honour of the Church of Constantinople with Old Rome, "but also because it by extension also implies the equality of honour of all local churches throughout the world." This canon "was a corrective step against the pyramid

---

[37] Dositheus of Jerusalem, ibid., pp. 366-367.

[38] Rallis and Potlis, *Syntagma: A Collection of the Divine and Holy Canons*, vol. II, p. 706.

Western "global" ecclesiology, which was expressed in the previous council of 869-870 and according to which the only truly local church in the foregoing sense of catholicity is the Church of Rome, which is identified with the global Church, and the only essential bishop is the Pope of Rome."[39]

## The Filioque

The second point that concerned this important council that we are studying is the question of the *Filioque*, the addition introduced by the Franks into the Symbol of Faith, that the Holy Spirit proceeds as a hypostasis from the Father and the Son. The Frankish missionaries had introduced the *Filioque* into Bulgaria and that was why this topic was posed to the council. It is the "essentialist view of the Holy trinity, which has Neoplatonic roots... As a result, essentialism destroys the correct theology of the Holy Trinity since it destroys the fount of Divinity, which is the monarchy of the Father."[40]

This serious question was discussed during the sixth session, and it was decided to forbid this cacodoxy. At the suggestion of Emperor Basil who was attending, the council decided to condemn the *Filioque*, that is, the introduction, into the Symbol of Faith by the Franks, of the heretical teaching on the procession of the Holy Spirit from the Father and from the Son, which the Franks had introduced also in Bulgaria. The deacon and protonotary Peter, at the command of Saint Photius the Great, read the relevant decree which prescribed the keeping of the Symbol of Faith of Nicea and the complete defrocking of the clergymen that add or subtract spurious words into the Symbol of Faith, and also the anathematization of laymen that do this. More specifically, after the introductory lines, the decree of this Œcumenical Council states:

"We expel those whom they removed from the Church, but we embrace and regard worthy of reception those whom they declared as deserving honor and sacred respect as being men of the same faith or even teachers of piety. Thus believing and thus declaring

---

39   Fr. Philip Zymaris, ibid., pp. 57-58.
40   Ibid., p. 207.

regarding these things, we embrace with mind and tongue and declare to all people with a loud voice the Definition of the most pure faith of the Christians which has come down even to us from the beginning through the Fathers, subtracting nothing, adding nothing, changing nothing, falsifying nothing; for subtraction and addition, when no heresy is stirred up by the ingenious fabrications of the evil one, introduces condemnation of the uncondemnable and an inexcusable assault on the Fathers, but to change with falsified words the definitions of the Fathers is much worse than the foregoing. Therefore this holy and Œcumenical Council, embracing with divine longing and uprightness of mind the definition of the Faith that was from the beginning and considering it divine, therein also founding and erecting the firmament of salvation, is of this mind and cries out to all to proclaim."[41]

Thereupon the Symbol of faith was read, without the addition of the phrase "[proceedeth] and from the Son", and straightway the decree declares:

"Thus we believe; into this confession of the Faith were we baptised; through it the word of truth has shown every heresy to be shattered and destroyed. Those who are of this mind we call brothers and fathers and fellow-heirs of the heavenly commonwealth. But should someone dare to compose another exposition besides this sacred Symbol, which has come down even to us from our blessed and sacred fathers, and call it a Definition of faith, and thus steal for himself the dignity of the confession of those divine men and enfold it with his own inventions, and set it forth as a common lesson to the faithful or even to those returning from some heresy, and be so audacious as to utterly adulterate with spurious words or additions or subtractions the antiquity of this sacred and venerable Definition, in accordance with the decree that has been declared already before us by the holy and Œcumenical Councils, if he be one of the clergymen, we subject him to complete defrocking, and if he be of the laymen, we defer him to the anathema."[42]

---

41  Dositheus, ibid., p. 378 [sixth act].

42  Dositheus, ibid., p. 379.

The mention of laymen refers to Charlemagne, who introduced the *Filioque*, and to the clergymen and bishops of Charlemagne's jurisdiction, who introduced the Symbol of Faith with the *Filioque* into the divine services and disseminated it thus into Bulgaria as well.

After the reading of this decree, the entire "present sacred concourse cried out, 'Thus are we all minded, thus do we believe, into this confession were we baptised and vouchsafed the priestly rank. Them who are otherwise minded, in violation of these things, we regard as enemies of God and of the truth. Should someone dare to compose and set up another Symbol besides this one or to add or subtract, and be so bold as to declare it a Definition, he is condemned and cast away from all Christian confession. For to subtract or to add is to portray as imperfect the confession to the holy and consubstantial and undivided Trinity, which has been from the beginning to this very day. It convicts the apostolic tradition and the doctrine of the fathers. Should therefore someone arrive at such an end of mindlessness as to dare, as has been said above, to set up another Symbol and call it a Definition, or to make either an addition or a subtraction in the one handed down to us from the holy and œcumenical first great Council in Nicea, let him be anathema.'"[43]

In his notes on the minutes of the Eighth Œcumenical Council, Dositheus of Jerusalem writes that at this council it became clear that even in the Roman Church no addition had yet crept into the Symbol of Faith but was rather invented later. If the priests of Pope Nicholas were teaching in Bulgaria the procession of the Holy Spirit also from the Son, yet they were doing so "of their own mind and not by the order of the pope." This is evident from the fact that even at the council that Pope Hadrian had convened by his petition to the Emperor, against Photius, that is, at the council of 869-870, it was decreed that the Symbol remain without any innovation, and their representatives had not disagreed, just as "the representatives of Pope John" did not disagree "in this council."[44]

---

43  Dositheus, ibid., pp. 379-380.

44  Dositheus, ibid., p. 416.

Of course, here it must be noted that it was Charlemagne that introduced the addition into the Symbol of Faith at the Council of Aachen in 809 and imposed it upon the bishops of his realm, but was then met with the reaction of the Pope of Rome. Later, however, in 1009, when Sergius IV, who was a Francophile, became Pope of Rome, he introduced the *Filioque* into the Symbol of Faith, whereupon he was struck from the diptychs and so we get the final schism, that is the separation of the Church of Rome, of the Francolatins, from the Orthodox Church.

From the foregoing it is evident that there is no doubt the council of 879-880 preserves all the external and internal elements of an Œcumenical Council. That is because it was convened by an Emperor, just as all the Œcumenical Councils, a great Patristic figure, Saint Photius the Great, presided over it, bishops from all the churches and even the legates of the Pope participated in it, and the issues that it faced were serious ecclesiological, dogmatic, and canonical issues. That is why most interpreters and theologians describe this council as the Eighth Œcumenical, as aforementioned.

## 4. The *Filioque* and the Primacy of the Pope After the Council of 879-880

As we have seen, the council of 879-880 dealt with two serious issues among others, namely, the *Filioque* and Papal primacy. These are two issues that still concern our Church to this day in the theological dialogues. Papal primacy had been expressed by the earlier popes, whereas the *Filioque* had been introduced by the Franks despite the reaction of the Pope of Rome till 1009, the year on which it was introduced into the Church of Rome.

These two serious theological questions are dogmas for the Latins and for us heresies, which are also found in the great dogmatic theologian of Papism, Thomas Aquinas. For this reason we shall mention what Thomas Aquinas has to say on these two matters.

The doctrine of the Francolatins on the procession of the Holy Spirit from the Father and from the Son (*Filioque*) is found in the works of Thomas Aquinas. For instance, we see it in his work *Summa*

*Theologica*, where the matter is expounded in a speculative and complex way, truly bewildering.

To the thirty-sixth question of the first part and particularly in the second article entitled "Does the Holy Ghost proceed from the Son?", Thomas Aquinas answers in five objections that he himself poses. He begins his answer by stating that "it must be said that the Holy Ghost is from the Son." Then he uses complex syllogisms which it is not easy to follow and understand, having as their central point the claim that "it cannot be said that the divine Persons are distinguished from each other in any absolute sense." Connecting the Word with the intellect and the Holy Spirit with love, he then writes "that the Son proceeds by the way of the intellect as Word, and the Holy Ghost by way of the will as Love. Now love must proceed from a word. For we do not love anything unless we apprehend it by a mental conception. Hence also in this way it is manifest that the Holy Ghost proceeds from the Son."

At another point of the same question, he mentions that the Holy Spirit proceeds also from the Son, even if He is said to proceed only from the Father: "therefore when we say that the Holy Ghost proceeds from the Father, even though it be added that He proceeds from the Father alone, the Son would not thereby be at all excluded; because as regards being the principle of the Holy Ghost, the Father and the Son are not opposed to each other, but only as regards the fact that one is the Father, and the other is the Son."

At another point, Thomas Aquinas tries to justify why the Pope added the *Filioque* into the Symbol of Faith, even though the Fathers did not do so in the First and Second Œcumenical Councils. He writes, "In every council of the Church a symbol of faith has been drawn up to meet some prevalent error condemned in the council at that time. Hence subsequent councils are not to be described as making a new symbol of faith; but what was implicitly contained in the first symbol was explained by some addition directed against rising heresies." His train of thought concludes, "Therefore, because at the time of the ancient councils the error of those who said that the Holy Ghost did not proceed from the Son had not arisen, it was not necessary to make any explicit declaration on that point; whereas, later on, when certain errors rose up, another council [Council of Rome, under Pope Damasus] assembled in the west, the matter was explicitly defined by the authority of the Roman Pontiff, by whose authority also the ancient councils were summoned and confirmed. Nevertheless the truth was contained implicitly in the belief that the Holy Ghost proceeds from the Father."

In another answer, Thomas Aquinas claims that the view that the Holy Spirit does not proceed also from the Son was introduced by the Nestorians, and that this then influenced others later on, including Saint John Damascene, although according to the interpretation of some, he does not deny the *Filioque*: "The Nestorians were the first to introduce the error that the Holy Ghost did not proceed from the Son, as appears in a Nestorian creed condemned in the council of Ephesus. This error was embraced by Theodoric [sic] the Nestorian, and several others after him, among whom was also Damascene. Hence, in that point his opinion is not to be held. Although, too, it has been asserted by some that while Damascene did not confess that the Holy Ghost was from the Son, neither do those words of his express a denial thereof."[45]

In the thirty-seventh question of the first part, Thomas Aquinas deals with the topic "The name of the Holy Ghost—Love", including two articles. In the first article he poses the question, "Whether 'Love' is the proper name of the Holy Ghost?" Among other things he writes, "The name Love in God can be taken essentially and personally. If taken personally it is the proper name of the Holy Ghost; as Word is the proper name of the Son. To see this we must know that since as shown above (I:27:2-5), there are two processions in God, one by way of the intellect, which is the procession of the Word, and another by way of the will, which is the procession of Love; forasmuch as the former is the more known to us, we have been able to apply more suitable names to express our various considerations as regards that procession, but not as regards the procession of the will."

---

45  Translator's note: This English translation is taken from *The Summa Theologiæ of St. Thomas Aquinas*. Rev. 2nd ed. 1920. NewAdvent.org. 2017. 7 Nov. 2023 https://www.newadvent.org/summa/1036.htm.

Using the image of the relationship between lover and loved, he makes complex syllogisms, concluding, "It follows that so far as love means only the relation of the lover to the object loved, "love" and "to love" are said of the essence, as "understanding" and "to understand"; but, on the other hand, so far as these words are used to express the relation to its principle, of what proceeds by way of love, and "vice versa," so that by "love" is understood the "love proceeding," and by "to love" is understood "the spiration of the love proceeding," in that sense "love" is the name of the person and "to love" is a notional term, as "to speak" and "to beget."

His basic thought that the Holy Spirit is the bond of love between Father and Son is expressed as follows: "The Holy Ghost is said to be the bond of the Father and Son, inasmuch as He is Love; because, since the Father loves Himself and the Son with one Love, and conversely, there is expressed in the Holy Ghost, as Love, the relation of the Father to the Son, and conversely, as that of the lover to the beloved. But from the fact that the Father and the Son mutually love one another, it necessarily follows that this mutual Love, the Holy Ghost, proceeds from both. As regards origin, therefore, the Holy Ghost is not the medium, but the third person in the Trinity; whereas as regards the aforesaid relation He is the bond between the two persons, as proceeding from both."[46]

Besides the *Filioque*, Thomas Aquinas also concerned himself with papal primacy. He sets the primacy of the Pope in the global Church on a dogmatic basis, which means that it is not a primacy of honour but a primacy of authority, in which case it becomes a primarily dogmatic rather than canonical issue. More specifically, in his *Contra errores Graecorum*, Thomas Aquinas writes: "The error of those who say that the Vicar of Christ… does not have a primacy over the universal Church is similar to the error of those who say that the Holy Spirit does not proceed from the Son. For Christ himself, the Son of God, consecrates and marks her [the Church] as his own with the Holy Spirit, as it were with his own character and

---

46 Translator's note: This English translation is taken from *The Summa Theologiæ of St. Thomas Aquinas*. Rev. 2nd ed. 1920. NewAdvent.org. 2017. 7 Nov. 2023 https://www.newadvent.org/summa/1037.htm.

seal... And in like manner the Vicar of Christ by his primacy and foresight as a faithful servant keeps the Church Universal subject to Christ."[47]

Oliver Clèment characteristically writes that "'filioquism', which causes the basic privilege that belongs only to the person of the father to be shared with the Son, thus making the Spirit dependent on the Son with respect to His own hypostatic existence, contributed without a doubt to the increase of the institutional and authoritarian element in the Roman Church." Fr. Placid Deseille says that with this observation of his, Oliver Clèment was repeating what Thomas Aquinas had been claimed, since "it is manifest that Roman ecclesiology differs from the Orthodox one, and it is no surprise that even Thomas Aquinas here pointed to a trinitarian root."[48]

## Conclusion

In conclusion, the council of 879-880 has all the prerequisites for being called the Eighth Œcumenical. As such it has been accepted by the conscience of the Orthodox Church, because (among other things) it had as its president a great Father of the Church, Saint Photius the Great, it was convoked by an emperor, all local churches were present, even the Church of Rome, and it also dealt with serious theological and ecclesiological issues, and it was this council that recognised the council of 787 as the Seventh Œcumenical.

The problem today is that the Popes of Rome do not reckon the council of 879-880 as the Eighth Œcumenical, but in its stead they have the council of 869-870, which condemned Saint Photius the Great. For some two centuries the council of 869-870 lay forgotten, and it was only in the eleventh century that Pope Gregory VII (1073-1085) first mentions this council. In fact, towards the end of the

---

[47] Translator's note: This English translation is taken from chapter 32 of Aquinas, Thomas. *Contra errores Graecorum*. Internet Archive: Wayback Machine. 2009. 7 Nov. 2023 https://web.archive.org/web/20090808081714/http://www.op-stjoseph.org/Students/study/thomas/ContraErrGraecorum.htm.

[48] Archimandrite Placid Deseille, *Ἡ πορεία μου πρὸς τὴν Ὀρθοδοξία* [*My journey to Orthodoxy*], transl. Archim. Symeon Koutsas, Akritas Publications, 2nd reprint 1999, pp. 105-106.

eleventh century "chroniclers begin to mention this council."[49] We, however, the contemporary Orthodox, stop counting Œcumenical Councils at the Seventh Œcumenical Council and still do not include this council among the Œcumenical, even though for the Church's consciousness it is Œcumenical, as explained above. Will we tolerate this? Ought we not to propose to the Pan-Orthodox Council that we recognize this important council as the Eighth Œcumenical, as many Fathers and teachers of the Church have done?

Regarding the hesychastic councils of the 14th century, and especially the council of 1351, which truly has the characteristics of an Œcumenical Council, because not only was it convoked by an emperor and had as its protagonist the great Father of the Church Saint Gregory Palamas, but at the same time it also faced and essentially condemned the heretical cacodoxy of *actus purus*, and may be termed the Ninth Œcumenical Council, the Reverend Metropolitan of Gortyna and Megalopolis and dear brother in Christ Jeremiah will give a report.

As I already mentioned at the beginning of the presentation, nothing prevents us as a local church from making a certain decision and offering it for discussion at a pan-Orthodox council or for inclusion among the topics for discussion at the Great and Holy Council that will be convoked—provided, of course, that this is possible, given that the list of topics for discussion has been decided.

I tried briefly to present the seriousness of this theological and ecclesiastical matter, and I thank the Holy Synod [i.e. the Standing Synod] for deciding to discuss this matter at the full Synod of the Hierarchy, as I also thank you once again for the honour of assigning to me the *examination* of this matter, although all hierarchs present are knowledgeable on these matters, especially those who work academically and confessionally on these serious issues.

---

49   Bishop of Abydos Cyril Katerelos, ibid., p. 306.

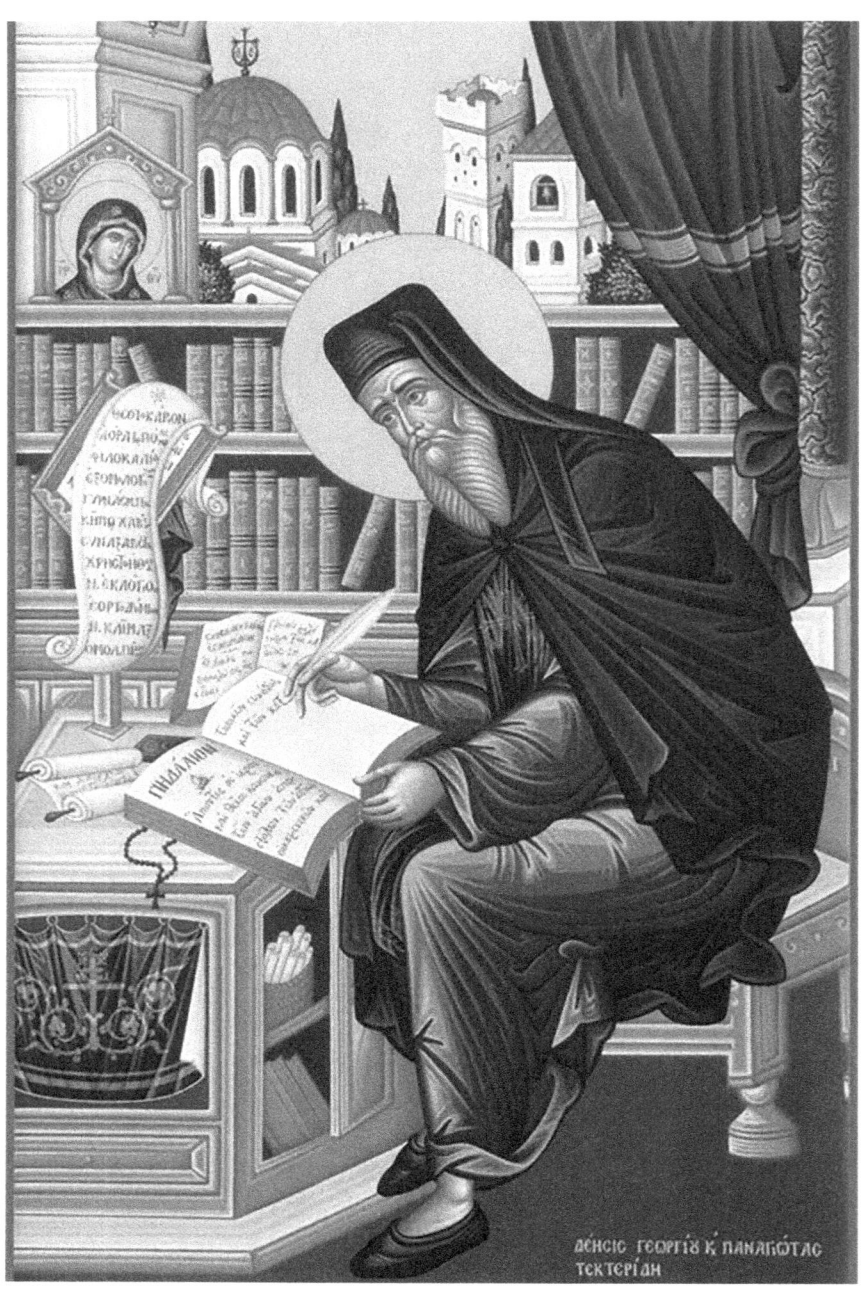

Saint Nikodemos the Hagiorite

# CRITERIA
## of the Œcumenicity of a Council

**Saint Nikodemos the Hagiorite**
"I find some four characteristic features of Œcumenical Council…

"The chief distinguishing feature of all Œcumenical Councils is the fact that they are convoked at the behest, not of the Pope or of such and such a patriarch, but by imperial orders.

"Second, that there be discussion concerning the Faith, and thereafter the exposition of a decision and a dogmatic decree [horos], which followed every single one of the Œcumenical Councils…

"Third, that all dogmas and canons laid out thereby be Orthodox, pious, and concordant with the divine Scriptures or the previous Œcumenical Councils…

"Fourth and last, that all Orthodox patriarchs and prelates of the Catholic Church agree and accept everything that has been decreed and ordained by the Œcumenical Councils, either by their personal presence or by their own legate or, in the absence of such a representative, by their letters."[50]

---

50 Saint Nikodemos the Hagiorite, *The Rudder* (Chicago IL: The Orthodox Christian Educational Society, 1957), pp. 155-156.

**Professor Fr. John Romanides**

"The Nine Roman Œcumenical Councils were convened by the Roman Emperor, beginning with Constantine the Great, in coordination with the Roman Patriarchates of Elder Rome, New Rome, Alexandria, Antioch and finally Jerusalem by 451. These Councils are (1) Nicea 325, (2) Constantinople 381, (3) Ephesus 431, (4) Chalcedon 451, (5) Constantinople 553, (6) Constantinople 680, (7) Nicea 786/7, (8) Constantinople 879 and (9) Constantinople 1341. We have here Eight Œcumenical Councils which were promulgated as Roman Law by the signature of the Emperor after their minutes had been signed by the Five Roman Patriarchates and their Metropolitans and bishops. Then we have the Ninth Œcumenical Council of 1341, whose minutes were signed by only Four Roman Patriarchates and countersigned by the Roman Emperor. Gone was now the Patriarchate of Elder Rome which had been forcefully captured by the Franks, Lombards, Germans and with the help of the Normans....

"The current idea among many Orthodox that an Œcumenical Council becomes finally official when it is recognized by a subsequent Œcumenical Council has no basis in Roman Law. Each such Council became Roman law the moment when its minutes were signed on the spot by the participating Patriarchal and Metropolitan Synods and countersigned by the Emperor himself. Heretics and their heresies were condemned on the spot and not at a subsequent Œcumenical Council. Their Creeds and *Horoi* became Roman law on the spot. ...

"So there are now Orthodox who even called themselves the Church of the Seven Œcumenical Councils. Most Orthodox are in a state of limbo about the Eighth and Ninth Œcumenical Councils. The Eighth Œcumenical Council of 879 simply condemned those who either "add to" or "subtract from" the Creed of 381 and also those who have not yet accepted the teaching of the Seventh Œcumenical Council about Icons. The Franks who were condemned were not mentioned at the time in order to allow them to reconsider. ...

"The Ninth Œcumenical Council of 1341 condemned the Platonic mysticism of Barlaam the Calabrian who had come from the West as a convert to Orthodoxy. Of course the rejection of the Platonic type of mysticism was traditional practice for the Fathers."[51]

**Œcumenical is the council**
1. which was convened by an Emperor of the Roman Empire with Œcumenical (pan-Roman), and of course also pan-Christian, range,
2. whose decisions were accepted by the entire Orthodox Church throughout the world, through the centuries,
3. whose decisions were formulated by a holy man (a man experiencing theosis),
4. whose decisions were signed by the Roman Patriarchates, and
5. which dealt with important theological issues.

---

51 Romanides, Fr. John. "Some Underlying Positions of This Website" Romanity.org. Accessed January 25th, 2023. http://romanity.org/htm/rom.00.en.some_underlying_positions_of_this_website.htm

Saint Nectarius of Pentapolis

# HISTORIC CONFIRMATIONS
## to the Council of 879-880 being Œcumenical

### Minutes of the Council

"Thus are we all minded, thus do we believe, into this confession were we baptised and vouchsafed the priestly rank. Them who are otherwise minded, in violation of these things, we regard as enemies of God and of the truth. Should someone dare to compose and set up another Symbol besides this one or to add or subtract, and be so bold as to declare it a Definition, he is condemned and cast away from all Christian confession. For to subtract or to add is to portray as imperfect the confession to the holy and consubstantial and undivided Trinity, which has been from the beginning to this very day. It convicts the apostolic tradition and the doctrine of the fathers. Should therefore someone arrive at such an end of mindlessness as to dare… to set up another Symbol and call it a Definition, or to make either an addition or a subtraction in the one handed down to us from the holy and œcumenical first great Council in Nicea, let him be anathema."[52]

"…It is fitting, along with all the reception and union of the Church of the Romans, by the intercession of our most holy patriarch Photius, to agree with us on this matter also…

---

52  Dositheus of Jerusalem, *Tome of Joy*, (Regopoulos: Thessalonica, 1995), pp. 379-380.

"And if anyone is not thus minded and does not recognise the holy and Œcumenical Seventh Council assembled the second time in Nicea, as the most God-fearing presbyter and cardinal has said, let him be anathema."[53]

"...those whom Photius our most holy patriarch shall subject to excommunication or defrocking or anathema in whichever sojourning, whether they be clergymen or laymen or of the archpriestly or priestly order, these the most holy Pope John and with him God's holy Church of the Romans is to hold in the same judgement of punishment, without any of the prerogatives belonging to the most holy throne of the Church of the Romans or to her president being at all innovated, neither now nor hereafter."[54]

"As for that our actions came to a good end, even if we should keep silent, the stones will cry out. Whoever does not walk by the acts of this holy and Œcumenical Council shall be separated from the holy and consubstantial Trinity."[55]

"...Therefore this holy and Œcumenical Council, embracing with divine longing and uprightness of mind the definition of the Faith that was from the beginning and considering it divine, therein also founding and erecting the firmament of salvation, is of this mind and cries out to all to proclaim."[56]

"God be praised, that the opinions and wills of all the most holy patriarchs have come together thus into one, and that by the common one-mindedness and peace all things undertaken and done by the holy and Œcumenical Council have ended well."[57]

---

[53] John Karmiris, *The Dogmatic and Symbolic Monuments of the Orthodox Catholic Church*, vol. 1, p. 227.

[54] John Karmiris, *The Dogmatic and Symbolic Monuments of the Orthodox Catholic Church*, vol. 1, p. 228.

[55] *Tome of Joy*, p. 367.

[56] Dositheus of Jerusalem, *Tome of Joy*, (Regopoulos: Thessalonica, 1995), p. 378.

[57] John Karmiris, *The Dogmatic and Symbolic Monuments of the Orthodox Catholic Church*, vol. 1, p. 367.

## Saint Nectarius of Pentapolis

"The Eighth Œcumenical Council is of great significance because it ratified the definition of Faith (*horos*) of the First and Second Œcumenical Councils and safeguarded the confession of Faith, having circumvallated it with a new fortified trench so that it remain impregnable, and also excommunicated and anathematized those that are of another and not of this mind, who do not confess this common Symbol, and restored ecclesiastical peace and unity between East and West. This council recognized the equality of the hierarchal offices of the bishops of Rome and Constantinople and the absolute authority of the Œcumenical Councils, to which even the Pope submitted by acknowledging the council's decisions. In this council Photius was triumphant, since in this council his struggles on behalf of the independence of the Church of the East were crowned with complete success and the truth of Orthodoxy, for which he had laboured so, reigned as king."[58]

## Professor Fr. George Metallinos

"But there is also the 8th Œcumenical Council. It is the Council of 879, under [Patriarch] Saint Photius the Great. The well-known professor of dogmatics, our teacher, John Karmiris of the Theological School of Athens, used to say that the Council of 879 under Saint Photius the Great is the last General Council of the Ancient Church before the Schism, with all the characteristics of an Œcumenical Council. This council condemns the Western alienation in the formulation of the Filioque, i.e. of the procession of the Holy Spirit not only from the Father, as our Christ says in the Gospel according to John, at 15:26—'which proceedeth from the Father'—but also 'from the Son.'

"The 8th Œcumenical Council is the council of 879, which condemns the Filioque, the addition of the phrase into the Symbol, and mainly them that introduced this addition into the Symbol, that is, the Frankish world and its leadership."[59]

---

58  Saint Nectarius, *Historical Study on the Causes of the Schism*, vol. I, Nectarius Panagopoulos Publications, p. 288-289.

59  Diocese of Piraeus. *The Divine Service of the Holy Eighth Œcumenical Council.*

## Professor Vlassios Pheidas

"By all means, the definition of the Council in Nicea, which the other holy and Œcumenical Councils also confirmed and built up, even this ought to be read in this great and Œcumenical Council as well."[60]

## Professor John Karmiris

[This Council] "constituted by 383 Fathers, both eastern and western, representing the five ancient patriarchates, presented (even according to the Roman Catholic theologian Hergenrother) such an imposing sight as had not been seen since the years of the Fourth Œcumenical Council in Chalcedon. Wherefore (he goes on to confess) this Council bears all the external characteristics of an Œcumenical Council. Thus it is no wonder at all that Theodore Balsamon, Nilus of Thessalonica, Nilus of Rhodes, Symeon of Thessalonica, Mark of Ephesus, Gennadius Scholarius, Dositheus of Jerusalem, Constantine Oikonomos, and others all considered it the Eighth Œcumenical; yet even the very Council characterized itself as Œcumenical in many passages of its minutes, as has moreover been done by Patriarch Euthymius and many others up to our contemporaries, Chrysostom Papadopoulos, F. Dvornik, and others."[61]

---

(Piraeus: Diocese of Piraeus, 2014), pp. 82-83.

60 From the Sixth Act of the Minutes of the Eighth Œcumenical Councils, quoted in V. Pheidas, *Ecclesiastical History*, vol. II, p. 133.

61 Despina D. Kontostergiou, *The Œcumenical Councils*, Pournaras Publications: 1997, p. 275-297.

Protopresbyter George Metallinos

Metropolitan Seraphim of Piraeus, Phalerum, Drapetsona & St. John Rendi

# PASTORAL ENCYCLICAL
## of the Most Reverend Metropolitan of Piraeus, Phalerum, Drapetsona & St. John Rendi
## SERAPHIM
## On the Occasion of the Institution of the Celebration of the Sacred Memory of the Holy 383 God-Bearing Fathers that Constituted the Eighth Œcumenical Council, On the Second Sunday of February

Dear fathers and brethren,

By the uncreated Grace of God, glorified in Trinity, and the intercessions of our Father among the saints Photius the Great, Archbishop of Constantinople and Equal to the Apostles, we celebrate today, on the first Sunday after the memory of Saint Photius, for the first time in our holy diocese the feast of the holy 383 God-bearing Fathers that constituted the VIII[th] (Eighth) Holy and Œcumenical Council in Constantinople in the years of our Lord 879-880. This feast will henceforth be celebrated annually in our holy diocese with the inspired holy service composed by Apostolos Papachrestou of blessed memory who now dwells in the heavenly courts, hymnographer and excellent servant of Orthodox Byzantine music and of the ecclesiastical typicon, whose memory be eternal, and another service composed just now at our request by the Reverend Nun Thecla of Saint Stephen's, upon whom, as also upon the Abbess of the Holy Monastery of Saint Stephen in Meteora, Nun Christonymphie, and her honourable company, we invoke the blessing of the Holy Fathers.

We Orthodox do not stop counting Œcumenical Councils at the VII[th] (Seventh) Holy and Œcumenical Council of A.D. 787 against the heretical and Christian-accusing iconoclasts; rather, we also reckon as Holy and Œcumenical Councils two other councils, first, the council of 879-880 under Saint Photius the Great, which is the Eighth Holy and Œcumenical Council, and second, the council of the year 1351 under Saint Gregory Palamas, archbishop of Thessalonica, which is the IX[th] (Ninth) Holy and Œcumenical Council.

The Eighth Holy and Œcumenical Council in the Hagia Sophia was convoked in Constantinople in the years 879-880 during the reign of Emperor Basil the Macedonian. Three hundred eighty-three holy and God-bearing Fathers from East and West participated, representing the five ancient Orthodox patriarchates, among whom was the Patriarch of Constantinople Saint Photius the Great, who presided over the council; the representative of the then Orthodox Pope of Rome John VIII, Peter the presbyter, along with Paul and Eugene; the representative of Patriarch Theodosius of Jerusalem, Elias the presbyter; the representative of Patriarch Michael of Alexandria, Cosmas the presbyter; and the representative of Patriarch Theodosius of Antioch, Bishop Basil of Martyropolis.

The council was called to put an end to the scandals that ensued between Easterners and Westerners regarding Bulgaria and for the unification of the bishops that had gone into schism on account of the expulsion of Ignatius, sometime Patriarch of Constantinople, and of the ordination of Saint Photius. The council also proclaimed the Œcumenicity of the Seventh Holy and Œcumenical Council.[62]

---

62 Saint Nikodemos the Hagiorite, *The Rudder*, (Regopoulos: Thessalonica 2003), pp. 361-366.

Five were the main topics discussed at the council, as follows: (a) the primacy of the Pope of Rome, (b) the offices in the Church and their interrelationship, (c) the local customs, (d) the immediate raising of a layman to the rank of bishop [consecutive ordination], and (e) the *Filioque*, i.e. the illegal and heretical addition of the procession of the Holy Spirit also from the Son.

The minutes of this council were published by the holy Dositheus, Patriarch of Jerusalem, in his book *Tome of Joy*, which was printed in Rimnik of Wallachia in September of 1705.

The council of A.D. 879-880 has all the characteristics of an Œcumenical Council and may be called the Eighth Œcumenical Council. It preserves all the external and internal elements of the Œcumenical Council.

This council is œcumenical and is so called because (a) it was convoked by Emperor Basil the Macedonian, (b) it was attended by representatives of all the patriarchates, with the great Patristic figure of Saint Photius the Great as its president and with representatives of the then Orthodox Pope of Rome John VIII, (c) it dealt with serious dogmatic, ecclesiological, and canonical issues, (d) its decisions follow the teaching of the holy Prophets, Apostles, and Fathers of the Church, i.e. they agree with the whole tradition of the Church, (e) all the Orthodox patriarchs and hierarchs of the Catholic Orthodox Church were in agreement, which is seen in their signatures on the decisions of the council, and which agreement is the constituent element that renders a council œcumenical, according to Saint Nikodemos the Hagiorite,[63] and (f) this council was described as œcumenical by many holy Fathers and teachers, such as Theodore Balsamon, Nilus of Thessalonica, Saint Nicholas Cabasilas, Nilus of Rhodes, Macarius of Ancyra, Saint Symeon of Thessalonicsa, Saint Mark Eugenicus of Ephesus, the venerable Joseph Bryennius, Saint Gennadius Scholarius, the holy Dositheus of Jerusalem, Constantine Oikonomos, and others, but also more recent ones, such as the Archbishop of Athens and all Hellas, His Eminence Chrysostom Papadopoulos of blessed memory, the Most Reverend

---

63  Ibid., p. 118.

Metropolitan of Naupactus and Saint Blaise, His Eminence Hierotheos,[64] the Most Reverend Metropolitan of Gortyna and Megalopolis, His Eminence Jeremiah,[65] the Most God-loved Bishop of Abydos, His Grace Cyril Katerelos,[66] the Reverend presbyter Fr. Philip Zymaris,[67] and others.

Carefully reading the minutes of this council, one realizes that the council itself had the consciousness of an Œcumenical Council, and it is thus titled by the Emperors, by Saint Photius the Great, by the legates of the then Orthodox Pope of Rome, and by its members. The term "Œcumenical" is attested dozens of times in the minutes. All the members of the council are conscious of being the continuation of the Seventh Holy and Œcumenical Council, whose œcumenicity they confirm. So, the fact that the Seventh Holy and Œcumenical Council was confirmed by the Eighth Œcumenical Council, along with other things, shows the seriousness of the latter.

On the basis of the above, it will be no novelty or innovation for us, as a Holy Diocese, as a local church, to accept the Council under Saint Photius the Great as œcumenical and to propose its official acceptance as such by the whole Orthodox Catholic Church, given that, according to the Orthodox Tradition, the council proclaims officially what already was, a council's œcumenicity, which is proven by the infallible conscience of the fullness of the Church.

---

64 Metropolitan of Naupactus Hierotheos, *On the Recognition of the Council Convoked in Constantinople in A.D. 879-880 as the Eighth Œcumenical*, Presentation to the Sacred Synod of Hierarchs of the Church of Greece (not read), October 2011.

65 Metropolitan of Gortyna Jeremiah, *On the Recognition of the Council Convoked in Constantinople in A.D. 1351 as the Ninth Œcumenical*, Presentation to the Sacred Synod of Hierarchs of the Church of Greece (not read), October 2011.

66 Bishop of Abydos Cyril, *Rome and Papal Primacy during the Patriarchate of Ignatius and Saint Photius (847-886): the Eighth Œcumenical Council of the Roman Catholic Church (869-870)*

67 Protopresbyter Philip Zymaris, *The Historical, Dogmatic, and Canonical Significance of the Council of Constantinople (879-880)*, doctoral thesis.

At this point it seems necessary to briefly mentioned two of the issues that concerned the Eighth Holy and Œcumenical Council, so that the significance of this Œcumenical Council might become apparent. These issues are first, the primacy of the Orthodox Pope of Rome, and second, the heresy of the *Filioque*.

A. The first point that concerned the Eighth Holy and Œcumenical Council has to do with the primacy of the Orthodox Pope of Rome. The discussions that took place during the council between Saint Photius the Great, the Eastern representatives, but also the representatives of the then Orthodox Pope of Rome John VIII clearly show that the Orthodox Pope of Rome has primacy within the Church, but with distinct ecclesiological boundaries, as these are defined by the 34th Apostolic Canon. In other words, he is first only according to seniority, within and not above the Church. According to this view, each bishop that does not keep the spirit of the Apostolic Canon places himself outside of the Church and is defrocked or excommunicated. The Popes of Rome are no exception.

Saint Photius the Great and the holy Fathers of this council supported primacy of honour (*presbeia timēs*) as a necessary ecclesiological principle for the preservation of the unity of the Church throughout the world. According to primacy of honour, however, this preservation of unity is clearly not understood as imposed by one *primus*, who is above the Church as an authority. This position is clearly expressed in an epistle of Saint Photius, in which he emphasises the Orthodox interpretation of the Gospel passage, "And I say also unto thee, That thou art Peter, and upon this rock I will build my church…" (Matthew 16:18-19). This interpretation leads to the crucial ecclesiological principle that each bishop is of equal honour as regards his priesthood. The Orthodox Pope of Rome, *not* the contemporary heresiarch, has the privilege of honour and must abide by the holy canons of the Church, while this privilege must be exercised within the spirit of the holy canons. This means that the Orthodox Pope of Rome has no jurisdiction in other ecclesiastical dioceses. When the Pope of Rome does not keep the holy canons and places himself above the Church, then he can be defrocked, as was done with Pope Nicholas I who was defrocked because he interfered with Constantinople and Bulgaria.

Very telling in this regard is the first sacred canon that this council drafted in its fifth act, which institutes the autonomy of each ecclesiastical diocese in matters of order and discipline. This holy canon accepts the conciliar system of governance and clarifies that the primacy of the Orthodox Pope of Rome is not a primacy of authority but a primacy of honour; in other words, the Orthodox Pope of Rome (*not* the current one, since he and his predecessors have fallen away into dread heresies from the year 1014) is not the head of the whole Church, he is not the fount of priesthood, and therefore he has no jurisdiction in other ecclesiastical dioceses. This holy canon is of crucial ecclesiological importance and is a corrective step against the pyramid Western "global" ecclesiology, which was expressed in the robber council of 869-870 and according to which the only truly local church (in the sense of 'catholic') is the Church of Rome, which is identified with the global Church, and the only essential bishop is the Pope of Rome.

B. The second point that concerned the Eighth Holy and Œcumenical Council was the issue of the *Filioque*, which the Franks introduced into the Symbol of Faith, i.e. that the Holy Spirit proceeds as a hypostasis from the Father and the Son.

The first and primary cause of the schism of 1054, that is, of the separation and severing of the ancient Patriarchate of the West, the heresy of Papism, from the One, Holy, Catholic, and Apostolic Orthodox Church, was the heresy of the *Filioque*. The *Filioque* is a terrible heresy, first of all (a) because it contradicts the most truthful word of Christ Himself, who said, "the Spirit of Truth, which proceedeth from the Father."[68] In other words, this is a blatant rejection of Christ God Himself. Second, (b) it is opposed to the Symbol of Faith of Nicea-Constantinople, which states, "I believe…and in the Holy Spirit, the Lord, the Giver of life, who proceedeth from the Father." In other words, this is rejection of

---

68 John 15:26.

both the 1st and the 2st Holy and Œcumenical Councils. Third, (c) it goes against the 7th holy canon of the 3rd Holy and Œcumenical Council, which forbids any addition or subtraction from the Symbol of Faith.[69] In other words, this is a rejection of the 3rd Holy and Œcumenical Council, as well. Fourth, (d) it destroys the relationship between the persons of the Holy Trinity and confuses the incommunicable hypostatic properties of the three persons. Fifth, (e) it lowers the Holy Spirit to the level of a creature, and sixth, (f) it introduces dyarchy into the Holy Trinity. Inasmuch as the Son is also a source of the Holy Spirit, we have two sources, two origins in the Holy Trinity, God the Father and the Son. Of course, behind the heresy of the *Filioque* there is hidden nothing but the other horrific heresy of the Pope of Rome, the pride, the arrogance, the infallibility, and the primacy of authority, that he alone should legislate on all things handed down by the Orthodox Church, according to the perceptive theology of Saint Gregory Palamas.[70]

This serious issue was discussed during the sixth session, and it was decided that this cacodoxy be forbidden. At the suggestion of Emperor Basil who was attending, the council decided to condemn the *Filioque*, that is, the introduction, into the Symbol of Faith by the Franks, of the heretical teaching on the procession of the Holy Spirit from the Father and from the Son, which the Franks had introduced also in Bulgaria.

In conclusion, the council of A.D. 879-880 under Saint Photius the Great is indeed the Eighth Holy and Œcumenical Council of the One, Holy, Catholic, and Apostolic Orthodox Church, and as such it has been accepted by the infallible conscience of the fullness of the Church. Today, the heresiarch popes of Rome do not number the council of A.D. 879-880 as the Eighth Holy and Œcumenical Council, but in its stead they number the robber council of 869-870, which condemned Saint Photius the Great,

---

[69] Saint Nikodemos the Hagiorite, *The Rudder*, (Regopoulos: Thessalonica 2003), pp. 173-176.

[70] Saint Gregory Palamas, *Apodictic Treatises on the Procession of the Holy Spirit*, (Uncut Mountain Press: 2022), Treatise 1.4, p. 73.

thus insulting the holy Equal-to-the-Apostles as a supposed "heresiarch".

Finally, we emphasize that we consider it indisputably necessary the convocation of a Pan-Orthodox, Holy, and Great Council with the participation of all Orthodox patriarchs, archbishops, metropolitans, bishops, abbots, archimandrites, priests, monks, and lay theologians, which will conciliarly examine the question of the pan-Orthodox proclamation of the council under Saint Photius the Great as the Eighth Holy and Œcumenical Council.

It is in fact singularly unacceptable for us, on the one hand, to consider Saint Photius the Great and Equal-to-the-Apostles as patron and guardian of the Church of Greece and of our Sacred Synod, not advance the process of submitting a proposal to proclaim the council of the year 880 as the Eighth Œcumenical, a council which pan-Orthodoxically and œcumenically justified Saint Photius the Great, and on the other hand to congregate and pray, entirely against the canons, together with the heretical papal religious parasynagogue and communion, which for obvious self-serving reasons accepts as the Eighth Œcumenical Council the robber council of 870, which as aforementioned insults Saint Photius the Great as a supposed "heresiarch".

Finally, it would be redundant to mention that the above certainly bothers and "burns" the demon of pan-heretical, syncretistic, inter-Christian ecumenism and as many as go along with him.

With prayers,<br>
THE METROPOLITAN<br>
Seraphim of Piraeus

Image of the Eighth Œcumenical Council from the Greek Service Book

# The Divine Service
## of the Holy Eighth Œcumenical Council

### Convoked in Constantinople
### In the Years of Our Lord 879-880

Composed by the reverend Nun Thecla of Saint
Stephen's Monastery in the Holy Meteora

*Chanted on the first Sunday of the Month of February*

First published in Piraeus of Greece by the holy
Metropolis of Piraeus
in the Year of our Lord 2014 and now seeing the Light
of Publicity for the first Time in English

———————————

*Translated from the original Greek by Gregory Heers
and edited by Monk Silouan*

In the United States of America
*at the Uncut Mountain Press*
in the Year of our Lord 2024 the Month of February

St. Photius the Great, President of the Eighth Œcumenical Council

# THE SERVICE OF THE HOLY EIGHTH ŒCUMENICAL COUNCIL

**Chanted on the 1st Sunday of the month of February. A composition of Nun Thecla of Saint Stephen's.**

## In Vespers

On the evening of Saturday, after the Proëmial Psalm, we chant "Blessed is the man." For Lord, I have cried, we stop at 10 verses and chant 4 Resurrectional Stichera and for the Holy Fathers six.

Stichera of the Fathers.
Tone Plagal II. *Having laid up all their hope.*

Zealously and eagerly · the blameless, true Faith defending, · the Eighth Œcumenical · Council did the God-inspired Fathers convocate. · Bringing down the ruinous, · strange and foreign dogmas, · they rebuilt the everlasting bounds, · they raised a bulwark new, · and in their great wisdom they kept intact · the Orthodox confession, · free from any damage of heresies. · Keeping their deposit, · preserving it as precious heritage, · their conversation celestial · let us also imitate.

Having ratified the Creed, · the Symbol written by God's hand · and decreed in councils erst, · them that durst compose a different one or subtract ·or insert audaciously ·therein an addition, ·them the holy shepherds then declared ·condemned and cast away ·from the godly Body, the Holy Church; ·they rightly thus considered them ·enemies of God and the foes of Truth. ·Thus with fear and trembling, ·exactitude we keep in everything, ·lest we should fall into similar ·condemnation ruefully.

Since the prelates of the West ·yet held the Orthodox mindset, ·standing in the council's midst, ·they agreed with all the writs that were then decreed; ·nonetheless, thereafterward ·by the fiend's delusion, ·they spewed forth a sordid blasphemy ·against the Holy Ghost, ·falling under their own anathema, ·forled by their severe mistake, ·clearly having rendered themselves fordeemed ·by self-condemnation. ·Preserve, therefore, the Holy Church unharmed ·by their corruption and injury, ·honourable Hierarchs.

Other hymns.
Same Tone. *Ere the morning star.*

Those who think that the Holy Ghost proceedeth ·from the Son have fallen from truth to falsehood; ·for sithence they foolishly ·did not accept Christ's witness, ·scorning the teaching of the Fathers, ·do they shamelessly blaspheme ·'gainst the all-holy, consubstantial, ·indivisible Threeness. ·Yet, O Master who dost will that all men ·be saved, do thou return e'en them to the Faith, O Lord, ·in true repentance, O Friend of Man.

Primacy of honour but not of power · neither of authority to the bishop · of the Elder Rome, who was · still Orthodox at that time, · this Council did indeed acknowledge, · thus upholding the order · within the Church, but never seeing · him as fount of all priesthood. · For the God-Man is our one and only · Great Hierarch and Mediator eternally · before the Father; we have none else.

Photius, thou president of the council, · with the other right godly-minded bishops, · enlightened in intellect · by uncreated splendor, · rightly theologising, did ye · then denounce Latin dogmas · as gravely false, deluded trifles · of a mind deep in darkness. · Do ye therefore supplicate the Saviour · that we may never walk by our own opinion · but by your teachings, O Saints of God.

### Glory. Tone Pl. I.

O Comforter, · Thou who spakest in the Prophets, the Apostles, · and the Doctors of the Church, · who abidest forevermore with us, · and into all truth guidest us: · Thou also call'dest the Fathers · to the Eighth Œcumenical Council · and through them confirm'dest anew · the Faith once delivered to the Saints, · condemning as enemies of God and of the Truth · those that were of another mindset. · Do Thou Thyself, O Heavenly King, · even now confirm us in Orthodoxy, · and by Thine uncreated grace hallow us.

Both now. Dogmatic Theotokion.
Then the Entrance, *O Joyous Light*, the Prokeimenon of the day, and the following Readings:

### The reading is from the Book of Deuteronomy (1:8-11, 15-17)

Thus said Moses to the sons of Israel: Behold, I have delivered the land before you; go in and inherit the land, which I sware to your fathers Abraham and Isaac and Jacob, to give it to them and to their seed after them. And I spake to you at that time, saying: I shall not be able to bear you by myself. The Lord your God hath multiplied you, and behold, ye are today as the stars of heaven for multitude. The Lord God of your fathers add to you a thousandfold more than ye are, and bless you as He hath spoken to you. So I took of you wise and understanding and prudent men, and I set them to rule over you as rulers of thousands, and rulers of hundreds, and rulers of tens, and instructors for your judges. And I commanded your judges at that time, saying: Hear causes between your brethren, and judge justly between a man and his brother, and the stranger that is with him. Thou shalt not have respect to persons in judgment, thou shalt judge small and great equally; thou shalt not shrink from before the person of a man, for the judgment is God's.

### The reading is from the Book of Deuteronomy (10:14-21)

Thus said Moses to the sons of Israel: Behold, the heaven, and the Heaven of heaven, belong to the Lord thy God, the earth and all things that are therein. Yet the Lord chose your fathers to love them, and above all nations, as at this day He chose you out of their seed after them. Therefore, ye shall circumcise the hardness of your heart, and ye shall stiffen your neck no more. For the Lord our God, He is God of gods, and Lord of lords, the great, and strong, and terrible God, Who doth not respect persons, nor will He by any means accept a bribe; executing judgment for the stranger and orphan and widow, and He loveth the stranger, to give him food and raiment. Thou shalt fear the Lord thy God, and Him only shalt thou serve, and to Him shalt thou cleave, and shalt swear by His name. He is thy boast, and He is thy God, Who hath wrought for thee these great and glorious things, which thine eyes have seen.

### The reading is from the Prophecy of Jeremiah (11:18-23, 12:1-5, 14-15)

O Lord, teach me, and I shall know: then I saw their doings. But I as an innocent lamb led to the slaughter, knew not: against me they devised an evil device, saying, Come and let us put wood into his bread, and let us utterly destroy him from off the land of the living, and let his name be remembered no more. O Lord, that judgest righteously, trying the reins and hearts, let me see Thy vengeance upon them, for to Thee I have declared my cause. Therefore thus saith the Lord concerning the men of Anathoth, that seek my life, that say, Thou shalt not prophesy at all in the name of the Lord, but if thou dost, thou shalt die by our hands: behold, I will visit them: their young men shall die by the sword; and their sons and their daughters shall die of famine: and there shall be no remnant left of them: for I will bring evil upon the dwellers in Anathoth, in the year of their visitation. Righteous art Thou, O Lord, that I may make my defense to Thee, yea, I will speak to Thee of judgements. Wherefore doth the way of the wicked prosper? that all that deal very treacherously are flourishing? Thou hast planted them, and they have taken root; they have begotten children, and become fruitful; Thou art near to their mouth, and far from their reins. But thou, O Lord, knowest me; Thou hast proved my heart before Thee; purify them for the day of their slaughter. How long shall the land mourn, and the grass of every field wither, for the wickedness of them that dwell therein? The beasts and birds are utterly destroyed; because they said, God shall not see our ways. Thy feet run, and they cause thee to faint. For thus saith the Lord concerning all the evil neighbours that touch mine inheritance, which I have divided to my people Israel; Behold, I will draw them away from their land, and I will cast out Judah from the midst of them. And it shall come to pass, after I have cast them out, that I will return, and have mercy upon them, and will cause them to dwell every man in his inheritance, and every man in his land.

## For the Entreaty.

### Idiomelon. Tone IV.

Lord Jesus Christ, our God before the ages, · One of the Consubstantial and Indivisible Trinity, · who for us becamest a man and callest all unto salvation, · Thou art the Good Shepherd, · who layest down Thy life for the sheep: · Thee do we suppliate, abundantly Merciful one: ·preserve Thy flock from every heresy ·and from the evils that are threatening it now. · Turn back in repentance those wandering astray, · to those not knowing Thee reveal Thyself, · and grant us the unity of the Faith, · that there may be one flock, · glorifying Thee, the One Shepherd, unto ages of ages.

### Glory. Tone Pl. I.

O Christ our God, · the Vine of Life, · whereon the Father grafted the Church · and watereth her everflowingly · by the life-bearing streams of the Spirit's Grace: · We pray Thee, O Master and Friend of Man: · keep us ever rooted in Thee, · Orthodox in faith and working Thy salvific commandments; ·that the Heavenly Husbandman not remove us as fruitless branches, · but purifying in repentance, He show us forth as fruitful, bearing abundant fruit of holiness.

### Both now. Theotokion.

We the faithful bless thee, O Virgin Theotokos, and we glorify thee, as is meet and proper: O unshaken city, impregnable battlement, invincible protection, and sheltering refuge of our souls.

## For the Aposticha.

Stichera of the Resurrection from the Octoëchos, and for the Fathers the following, if ye will.

### Tone I. *O all-lauded Martyrs.*

The dearest disciple of the Lord ·bids the faithful not converse ·neither to mingle with heretics; ·so, with deluded men ·how is it permitted ·for us to communicate, ·supposedly for love's sake? But by his prayers, ·O Christ, implant Thy fear ·in the hearts of us who worship Thee, ·that we not stray far from Thy commands of life.

> Verse: Blessed art thou, O Lord, the God of our Fathers, and praised and glorified is Thy Name unto the ages.

The Eighth Council's Fathers truly wise, ·speaking with great clarity, ·have proven heralds of godly truth, ·condemning heresies ·and the Latin dogmas. ·Wherefore let us flee in haste ·from those who overshadow the sacred truth ·by machinations new, ·paying no heed to the Fathers' words ·for the sake of pleasing this conceited world.

> Verse: Gather together unto Him His holy ones who have established His covenant upon sacrifices.

The serpent and source of vice expelled ·from noetic Paradise ·the cacodox, and he exiled them ·to an unwatered land, ·void of Godly rivers, ·where the tares of heresy ·and eke the thorns and thistles of wickedness

·flourish abundantly; ·so, obediently let us work ·in the fertile field of Orthodoxy.

Glory. Tone Pl. II.

Fathers thrice-blessed, ·being replete with the gifts of the Spirit, ·ye were shown forth as Christ-imitating shepherds of the Church, ·and as watchful wardens of the dogmas divine. ·From the ends of the earth, O all-glorious ones, having come together in the Eighth Holy Council, at the bidding of the Heavenly King ·and in the presence of the earthly one, ·ye confirmed the Orthodox confession ·contained in the divinely-written Symbol, ·showing this to be the foundation of salvation; ·and casting under the anathema of heresy ·those that dare make thereto any change or alteration, ·ye secured it by a new fortification, ·whereover no enemy can climb. ·Beseech ye in our behalf, ·all-brilliant luminaries of the Church, ·that we may keep with fear and reverence the Holy Tradition, ·allowing not treacherous foes to capture, ·in the sleep of heartsease, our most precious inheritance.

Both now. Theotokion.

O Theotokos, thou art the true vine that hath blossomed forth the Fruit of Life. Thee do we supplicate: Intercede, O Lady, together with the Apostles and all the Saints that our souls find mercy.

Now lettest Thou Thy servant. Trisagion.<br>
Dismissal Hymns. The Resurrectional; then, of the Fathers.

### Tone Pl. I. *Let us worship the Word.*

Of the Eighth Œcumenical Council let us praise ·the holy, God-bearing Fathers with songs of praise and of thanks, ·those defenders and revealers of the sacred Truth; ·for they have kept and guarded well ·and have handed down to us without any spot or blemish ·the Faith divinely proclaiméd, ·the foundation of theosis.

### Glory. Another.
### Tone I. *While Gabriel was saying.*

The Fathers of the Eighth Œcumenical Council, ·having proven pillars of Truth and destroyers of delusion, ·imparted to us, whole and intact, ·the great and priceless treasure of our Faith; ·for which cause, as ones indebted, we sing your praise, ·while blessing the Lord our Saviour: ·Glory to Him that called and gathered you. ·Glory to Him that strengthened you. ·Glory to Him that rendered radiant your Godly intellect.

### Both now. The Theotokion of the Tone.

## In Matins

*After the Six Psalms, the Dismissal Hymns as in Vespers.*

*The Sessional Hymns.*

*After the first reading, a Resurrectional.*

### Glory. Of the Fathers.
Tone I. *The soldiers standing guard.*

The Fathers of the Eighth Œcumenical Council · with pious reverence do we honour in praises, · while offering the Trinity songs of gratitude; for through them · hath He raised around our purest faith an entrenchment ·unassailable unto the ages of ages, ·to all of its enemies.

### Both now. Theotokion.

We know thee as the Mother of God, who are truly · a virgin even after thy childbirth, O Maiden; ·with longing, we flee in faith to thy goodness and sympathy. · For we sinners have thee as our certain protection, ·and as our salvation in distress and temptations, ·thou only all-blameless one.

*After the second reading, a Resurrectional.*

### Glory. Of the Fathers.
Tone IV. *Thou who wast raised up.*

The lightsome stars that bear the light of Orthodoxy, ·of whom the brightest is the star of the morning, ·

beholder of the Uncreated Light of the Three, ·Equal to Apostles, Photius, ·have conducted a brilliant ·triumph against darkness-deep ·with this the Eighth Council; ·so let us therefore walk forevermore ·in the light of Truth, by their interceding prayers.

Both now. Theotokion.

O Theotokos, we shall not cease from speaking ·of all thy mighty acts, all we the unworthy ones; ·for if thou hadst not stood to intercede for us, ·who would have delivered us ·from such numerous perils? ·Who would have preserved us all ·until now in true freedom? ·O Lady, we shall not turn away from thee; ·for thou dost always save thy servants from all manner of grief.

After the third reading, a Resurrectional.

Glory. Of the Fathers.
Tone IV. *Joseph was amazed.*

With a heart sincere and pure ·and with a burning soul's desire, ·with a mind captive of God, ·the famed expounders of the Truth ·at the Eighth Council, respecting the Church Tradition, ·truly have done well, setting first of all ·the same as the foundation of holiness, ·and intimating that this is the finest measure, ·this they bequeathed perfect unto us; ·wherefore with prudence let us embrace this ·sacred, holy deposit.

*Both now. Theotokion.*

Joseph was amazed to see · that which transcended nature's bound, ·for without seed, thou, O Maid, ·didst both conceive and bear a Child. · And he remembered the rod of Aaron, · the dew upon the fleece, · and the unburning bush · which was not consumed, · though it was all aflame. · Thus, thy protector and betrothèd cried, · as he bare witness before the priests: · A Virgin beareth, and after childbirth, · still remaineth a Virgin.

*Then the Blameless (Psalm 118), the Evlogitaria, and the Hypakoë.*

*The Hymns of Ascent in the Tone of the week.*

*The Matinal Gospel. Then,* Let us who have beheld the Resurrection of Christ.

*The Fiftieth Psalm, and the rest.*

*Then we say the Canons, of the Resurrection with its Heirmos and of the Fathers.*

*The Canon of the Holy Fathers.*
*Tone Pl. II. Ode I.* When Israel walked on foot.

Come, let us praise the initiates of the one · Consubstantial Trinity, · for they piously preserved · the True Faith, and this without a change, · perfect, blameless, incorrupt, ·they handed down to us.

The Church's reverend dogmas were written down · by the holy Spirit's quill; · Wherefore in the synod's midst ·did the God-inspired fathers chide ·and condemn as grave delusion every change thereto.

Strangers to God on account of their ill belief, · the most dread anathema, ·the conciliar decree, ·did the Latins bring upon themselves. · Understanding not at all, ·they lost the grace of God.

### Theotokion.

Since we confess thee as Mother of God in truth, ·being faithful Orthodox, ·let no storm of doubting thoughts ·fall upon us, O Immaculate, ·though in matters of the Faith ·we have been negligent.

### Ode III. *There is none holy as art Thou.*

Inclining pleasantly their ear · to the serpentine counsel, · thus the Latins departed ·far from God lamentably ·and strayed afar from the Church, ·the noetic, spiritual Paradise.

O holy Photius, thou wise · president of the Council, · thou resistedst with shrewdness · domination by the West, ·preserving thereby the Church ·of the East as perfectly autonomous.

O holy Fathers of the Eighth, ·following ever after · the Apostles' tradition, ·ye have clearly proven that ·in the succession thereof ·not a portion ·falleth to the Latins' lot.

### Theotokion.

O Lady, intercede for us, ·that we may ever hymn thee ·and may worship with pure heart ·God the Holy Trinity; · and that we steadfastly hold ·the confession of the Holy Orthodox Faith.

### Sessional Hymn of the Fathers.
### Tone II. *O fervent advocate.*

Extolling faithfully the Fathers most excellent · of the Eighth Council, intently let us follow them, ·keeping what they handed down, ·and abide in the most blameless Faith, ·for this is the one and only way ·unto the desirèd end of theosis.

### Theotokion.

O fervent advocate, invincible battlement, · fountain of mercy, and sheltering retreat for the world, · earnestly we cry to thee, ·Lady Mother of God, hasten thou ·and save us from all imperilment, ·for thou alone art our speedy protectress.

### Ode IV. *Christ is my power.*

In Godly-mindedness ·the Fathers have declared ·that to say that the Spirit eke from the Son ·doth proceed is heresy. ·So who could utter otherwise, ·contradicting with audacity?

The aweful mystery ·of the monarchical ·Threeness is by a foreign dogma blasphemed; ·for the Godhead's only Fount, ·the Father, is thereby denied ·and a diarchy is introduced.

A demon's finding is ·the Latins' added phrase ·in the Creed; for it changeth the idioms ·of distinct Hypostases ·of the monarchic, unconfused, ·and thrice luminous Divinity.

### Theotokion.

The Word assumed from thee ·the substance of us men ·by the eternal Father's goodwill, O Maid, ·Bride of God Immaculate, ·and by the coming of the Lord's ·Holy Spirit cobeginningless.

### Ode V. *With Thy divine light.*

The Spirit's connaturality ·with the Father, Son, by false a faith ·the West insulteth, degrading Him, ·one of the three Persons of the ·Monarchical God, ·one perfect, consubstantial, into an energy.

From heights of Heaven did Satan fall ·when he once desired to impose ·over the welkin-high clouds his throne. Wishing thus to sit o'er the firmament of the Church, ·the shepherd of the Latins hath now been exiled thence.

Thinking himself the distributor ·of the priesthood, the Heresiarch ·doth introduce a new heresy; ·for of course the Lord Jesus Christ ·is naturally ·the one and only giver of holy priesthood's gift.

### Theotokion.

From unclean passions deliver us · and from self-conceit, O spotless one, ·which hurl man into Hell's abyss, ·but by thine entreaties give thou ·humility's grace, ·which raiseth to theosis and to perfectedness.

### Ode VI. *Beholding the sea of life.*

Forsaking the only Truth, · the assembly of the West, ·entangled by the wiliness ·and deception of falsehood, slipt o'er the cliff ·and precipice leading down ·to perdition on account of many heresies.

Mistaken are they that think · that the Godhead's energies ·are but created; sithence thus ·both the path to theosis for mortal men ·is rendered impassible · and for creatures is God made unapproachable.

Empoisoned with heresy, · clearly doing away with the ·tradition of the Holy Church, ·even Baptism by triple immersion they ·abolished heretic'ly ·and by sprinkling or pouring they perform this rite.

### Theotokion.

Immaculate Maiden, thou · in thy womb conceiv'dest Christ, ·surpassing all of nature's laws, ·but according to nature wast thou conceived; · we say, therefore, that belief ·in thy spotless conception is delusional.

## The Kontakion. Tone IV. *On this day Thou hast appeared.*

At the Spirit's ordinance, ·from all the earth's ends ·the divine expositors ·of Truth assembled with one mind ·in the Eighth General Gathering, ·fighting to safeguard the Faith of the Orthodox.

## The Oikos.

The beacons of the Church, their hearts all ablaze with yearning for Christ, shewed the confession of the right Faith to be the only sure foundation of longed-for theosis, and every addition, subtraction, or alteration of the Synods' Symbol to be delusion and all-destroying heresy. Wherefore the divine expositors of the Truth befittingly convicted the Latins' unsound beliefs as blasphemous teachings, rejectaneous and foreign to the Faith of the Orthodox.

## The Synaxarion.

On the same day, we commemorate the three hundred and eighty-three God-bearing Fathers who assembled in Constantinople in the Holy Eighth Œcumenical Council, under Emperor Basil I the Macedonian, during the Patriarchy of Photius, Archbishop of Constantinople New Rome, the Great, in the eight hundred and seventy ninth and eight hundred and eightieth years of our Lord (A.D. 879-880).

## Couplet.

The Fathers proved in Council the procession
Of the Ghost from eke the Son to be delusion.

### Another.

The One Church gave to the Bishop of Rome
The privilege of honour but not of authority.

This council was convened in Constantinople, in the most sacred temple of the Wisdom of God, in the eight hundred and seventy ninth and eight hundred and eightieth years of our Lord (A.D. 879-880), by the Emperor of the Romans Basil I the Macedonian, with the participation of the five Elder Patriarchates. The Patriarch of Constantinople New Rome Photius the Great headed the Holy Fathers gathered there, and representatives of the Pope of Rome John VIII (who was still Orthodox), Peter the Presbyter, Paul, and Eugene; the representative of Patriarch Theodosius of Jerusalem, Elias the presbyter; the representative of Patriarch Michael of Alexandria, Cosmas the presbyter; and the representative of Patriarch Theodosius of Antioch, Basil bishop of Martyropolis, participated as well.

In this Eighth Œcumenical Council, the Holy Fathers, inspired by the Holy Spirit and following the foregoing wise Teachers and Saints of the Church, confirmed the decisions of the Seventh Œcumenical Council and condemned as heresy the belief that appeared in the Church of the West concerning the procession of the All-Holy Spirit not only from the Father, as saith our Lord Jesus Christ in the Gospel and as the divinely inspired Fathers dogmatised in the former councils and expounded in the Symbol of Faith, but also from the Son. Furthermore, they condemned those that are otherwise minded, in violation of the things instituted by the Holy

Councils, and those that dare make addition or subtraction in the Divine Symbol, as heretics, enemies of God and of the truth, and rejectaneous from the Church.

Moreover, the God-bearing Fathers also condemned the claim of the Bishop of Rome to primacy of authority over the Church, who was saying that he is the source of the priesthood. This, however, especially thanks to the strong and ingenious leadership of the most wise Patriarch Photius, proved to be heresy; wherefore only a primacy of honour was acknowledged to him, the independence of the Eastern Church being thus preserved.

Likewise, the council brought peace to the Church, putting an end to the troubles that had arisen between East and West on account of Bulgaria, uniting the bishops that had gone into schism over the dismissal of Ignatius, sometime Patriarch of Constantinople, and the ordination of Saint Photius in his stead, and thus preserving Orthodoxy in the Church. Certain others matters were also discussed, such as the offices in the Church, consecutive ordination (that is, the immediate raising of a layman to the rank of bishop), and local customs.

By the intercessions of the Holy Fathers, O Christ our God, keep us steadfast in the Orthodox Faith and save our souls. Amen.

### Ode VII. *An Angel made the furnace.*

Western blasphemy hath given birth to much and ill ·progeny, infallibility, ·the denial of the Chalice to the laity, ·the use of unleaven'd bread and thus ·deficient Liturgy, and more ·departures unto this day.

Inescapably the godly ethos will be changed ·following heresy's ill effects, ·sithence holiness is the fruiting of the Holy Ghost. ·The West by delusion hath thus been · completely separate from God ·and is of worldly-mind.

As a curelessly infected member, from the Church · by the sword of the Spirit the West ·did the healers cleave and they severed; how then shall we dare ·consider them as a healthy lung, ·since they will not accept to drink ·the remedy of return.

### Theotokion.

Silence the rhetóric , impious delusion that ·preacheth now opposite to the words ·of the Scriptures and the Apostles and the Fathers' choir · with intricate verbal intercourse, ·communing with the Westerners ·as if with brethren in Christ.

### Ode VIII. *From the flame.*

In the Holy Eighth Council gathered with one accord, ·the most ven'rable Shepherds made clear the Sacred Faith, ·first of whom the luciform ·Great father Photius, ·who confuted falsehood ·by virtue of the Truth's light.

With Saint Photius also the representatives ·of Pope John, namely, Peter, Paul, and Eugenius, ·made secure the boundaries · of the most holy Faith, · unto clear confutement ·of error to the ages.

The engodded assembly formeth a holy host, ·a great company gathered from all the East and West, ·from the land of Sion, from · Egypt and Antioch, · God the Word's revealers, ·the Christ-elected Shepherds.

## Theotokion.

With the love of the Holy Trinity smite thou us; ·set on fire our lukewarm spirit, O Maiden pure, ·that the perfect, spotless Faith ·trusted us by the Saints ·we may keep and treasure ·by sweat and blood and toil.

### Ode IX. *It is not possible for man.*

Possessing perfect the greatest gift of love, · as wild, savage wolves the wisest shepherds drave from the flock ·those believing otherwise, despite the august ·dogmas of all the Councils. ·Let us be not deceived; ·for familiarity with them is not a mark of love.

We cannot slothfully stand before the things ·divinely instituted by the Fathers conciliarly. ·For whoever walketh not in concord with them · shall be forever sundered ·from God the Trinity ·and a total stranger to the Church and rejectaneous.

There is no droplet of grace in any way ·in those whom from the tree of life the ax of delusion cut; · as the Œcumenical and Eighth Council saith ·clearly and most distinctly. ·How then the Westerners ·do we take to be a blossoming branch of the Church of Christ?

Dissolve the villainous, darksome sophistries ·of those who dare reject your resolutions inspired of God, ·Photius along with all the Shepherds most wise, ·and who are keenly striving ·to bring a union, ·but with unrepentant heretics. What an absurdity!

### Theotokion.

O blameless Maiden, beseech the Merciful ·and man-befriending God ·who took our nature from thy pure blood ·to establish us by grace, unchanging in the · Holy and Orthodox Faith, ·for no one but the ark ·of the Church possesseth and preserveth all the Truth of Faith.

### Exapostilarion. Tone III. *Thou who as God adornest.*

The steadfast, unswerving pillars ·of Orthodoxy as we praise ·the Fathers of the Eighth Council, ·faithfully treading in their steps, ·let us proceed after them in Faith, ·Orthodox also in our life.

### For the Praises.
### The Resurrectional hymns and the Holy Fathers'.
### Tone IV. *Thou who wast called from on high.*

From the inhabited world's ends assembled · in the Queen of Cities, O ·Fathers all-ven'rable, ·successors of Apostolic thrones, ·ye constituted ·a council full equal in authority ·to the seven former ones, ·bid by the Holy Ghost; ·and though thereafter the West declared · it as invalid, ·a robber council, with treacherous intent, ·yet by this council did ye bring about ·the good order andpeace and onemindedness ·and complete independence ·and security of the Church.

From the high summit of virtues having entered ·into the Thaborian ·Light, ye confirmed the Church, ·the ark of holiness, causing her ·to come to settle ·upon the mountain of dogmas right and true, ·where neither the deluge of ·heresies nor the streams ·and currents of this vain world can ·founder nor sink her. ·Rather, as she is the one eternal and ·the everlasting treasury of grace, · keeping in her the tablets of Law unharmed, ·she doth hallow the faithful ·that with steadfastness abide in her.

Faithfully following Orthodox Tradition, ·this ye clearly showed to be ·the base of théosis ·and deviation did ye convict ·as being delusion, ·alienating a man from grace divine. ·Wherefore, having shown to us ·the God-appointed mete, · O holy Teachers and God-seers, · beseech our Master, ·the Friend of Man, that we may not ever lose ·this precious treasure in the present age, ·so tempestous and dark, but keep hold of it ·as divine conversation's ·most infallible criterion.

Thine infatigable struggles do we honour, ·Photius the Greatest, and · thee do we celebrate; ·for in the Eighth Œcumenical · didst thou appear as · an undefeatable champion of Truth; ·for by grace and zeal and with ·thy theological ·and fearless tongue, robust intellect, ·and with thy wisdom, ·thou wast triumphant and most victorious ·over the blasphemous impiety. ·

Persecutions, therefore, insults and reproach, · as was to be expected, · on thy good confession put their seal.

### Glory. Tone II.

Keeping the all-sacred memory · of the divinely honoured Fathers of the Eighth Council, · Thee we glorify, Beginningless Trinity, our God. · For to the people that boasteth in Thee · and is rich with wealth inviolate, · even the Orthodox Faith, · Thou hast granted the Holy Councils, wherein Thou showest forth the Church · and Thy Truth Thou revealest. · This Eighth Council is Thy perfect gift also, · wherein Thou confirm'dest the decrees that were from the beginning · and didst once more establish them as a touchstone of the pure confession. · Wherefore we pray Thee, O Superessential Godhead: · enlighten us, that we may ever walk by the acts thereof, · lest we be found sundered from Thee, the Life of all.

### Both now.

Most blessed art thou…

### The Great Doxology.

Today is salvation come unto the world…

## In the Divine Liturgy

*The Typica, the Beatitudes of the Octoëchos, and from the Canon of the Holy Fathers the VI Ode.*

*The Epistle:* Son Titus, faithful is the word… *(Seek on the XI of October.)*

*The Gospel according to Matthew:* The Lord said unto his disciples, Ye are the light of the world… *(Seek on the XII of November.)*

*Magnificat.*

Glorious and noble Fathers, rejoice, ⸱ of the Eighth Council, ⸱for with wisdom did ye destroy ⸱abominable error ⸱by power of the Spirit, ⸱securing and safeguarding ⸱the boundaries of the Faith.

Couplets.

Fadres blisful, frið besecheþ
For þe Chirche, of fon biseged.

Fathers blissful, peace beseech
For the Church, by foes besieged.


Being come to this book's end,
Say a prayer for me, too, friend.

# UNCUT MOUNTAIN PRESS TITLES

## Books by Archpriest Peter Heers

Fr. Peter Heers, *The Ecclesiological Renovation of Vatican II: An Orthodox Examination of Rome's Ecumenical Theology Regarding Baptism and the Church*, 2015

Fr. Peter Heers, *The Missionary Origins of Modern Ecumenism: Milestones Leading up to 1920*, 2007

## The Works of our Father Among the Saints, Nikodemos the Hagiorite

Vol. 1: *Exomologetarion: A Manual of Confession*
Vol. 2: *Concerning Frequent Communion of the Immaculate Mysteries of Christ*
Vol. 3: *Confession of Faith*

## Other Available Titles

Elder Cleopa of Romania, *The Truth of our Faith*
Elder Cleopa of Romania, *The Truth of our Faith, Vol. II*
Fr. John Romanides, *Patristic Theology: The University Lectures of Fr. John Romanides*
Demetrios Aslanidis and Monk Damascene Grigoriatis, *Apostle to Zaire: The Life and Legacy of Blessed Father Cosmas of Grigoriou*
Protopresbyter Anastasios Gotsopoulos, *On Common Prayer with the Heterodox According to the Canons of the Church*
Robert Spencer, *The Church and the Pope*
G. M. Davis, *Antichrist: The Fulfillment of Globalization*
*Athonite Fathers of the 20th Century, Vol. I*
St. Gregory Palamas, *Apodictic Treatises on the Procession of the Holy Spirit*
St. Hilarion (Troitsky), *On the Dogma of the Church: An Historical Overview of the Sources of Ecclesiology*
Fr. Alexander Webster and Fr. Peter Heers, Editors, *Let No One Fear Death*
Subdeacon Nektarios Harrison, *Metropolitan Philaret of New York*
Elder George of Grigoriou, *Catholicism in the Light of Orthodoxy*
Archimandrite Ephraim Triandaphillopoulos, *Noetic Prayer as the Basis of Mission and the Struggle Against Heresy*
Dr. Nicholas Baldimtsis, *Life and Witness of St. Iakovos of Evia*
*On the Reception of the Heterodox into the Orthodox Church: The Patristic Consensus and Criteria*
Patrick (Craig) Truglia, *The Rise and Fall of the Papacy*
St. Raphael of Brooklyn, *In Defence of St. Cyprian*
*Orthodox Patristic Witness Concerning Catholicism*
Hieromartyr Seraphim Zvezdenskiy, *Homilies on the Divine Liturgy*

## Select Forthcoming Titles
Cell of the Resurrection, Mt. Athos, *On the Mystery of Christ: An Athonite Catechism*
*Minutes of the Eighth Œcumenical Council*
Georgio (Pachymeres), *Errors of the Latins*
Fr. George Metallinos, *I Confess One Baptism*, 2nd Edition
St. Maximus the Confessor, *Obscula: Theological and Polemical Works*
Fr. Peter Heers, *Going Deeper in the Spiritual Life*
Fr. Peter Heers, *On the Body of Christ and Baptism*
*Athonite Fathers of the 20th Century, Vol. II*

**This 1ˢᵗ Edition of**

## THE DIVINE SERVICE
### OF THE HOLY EIGHTH ŒCUMENICAL COUNCIL

written by Nun Thecla of Saint Stephen's Monastery in Metora, Greece, translated by Gregory Heers, and typeset in Baskerville, in this two thousand and twenty-fourth year of our Lord's Holy Incarnation, is one of the many fine titles available from Uncut Mountain Press, translators and publishers of Orthodox Christian theological and spiritual literature. Find the book you are looking for at

u n c u t m o u n t a i n p r e s s . c o m

**GLORY BE TO GOD
FOR ALL THINGS**

**AMEN.**

www.ingramcontent.com/pod-product-compliance
Lightning Source LLC
Chambersburg PA
CBHW061740070526
44585CB00024B/2748